Sylvia's Bridal Sampler
from
ELM CREEK QUILTS

The True Story Behind the Quilt ■ 140 Traditional Blocks

JENNIFER CHIAVERINI

Text copyright © 2009 by Jennifer Chiaverini

Artwork copyright © 2009 by C&T Publishing, Inc.

Publisher: Amy Marson

Creative Director: Gailen Runge

Editor: Teresa Stroin

Technical Editors: Teresa Stroin, Carolyn Aune, Sandy Peterson, Gailen Runge, and Ann Haley

Copyeditor/Proofreader: Wordfirm Inc.

Cover Designer: Christina Jarumay

Book Designer: Aliza Shalit, AK Design

Production Coordinator: Kirstie L. Pettersen

Illustrator: Richard Sheppard

Photography by Christina Carty-Francis and Diane Pedersen of C&T Publishing, Inc.,
unless otherwise noted

Published by C&T Publishing, Inc., P.O. Box 1456, Lafayette, CA 94549

Library of Congress Cataloging-in-Publication Data

Chiaverini, Jennifer.

Sylvia's Bridal Sampler from Elm Creek quilts : the true story behind the quilt : 140 traditional blocks
/ Jennifer Chiaverini.

  p. cm.

Includes index.

Summary: "This book contains the patterns for the 140 traditional blocks that make up the quilt,
Sylvia's Bridal Sampler, that was featured in one of Ms. Chiaverini's previous novels"--Provided by
publisher.

ISBN 978-1-57120-655-8 (paper trade : alk. paper)

1. Patchwork--Patterns. 2. Quilting--Patterns. 3. Patchwork quilts. I. Title.

TT835.C459 2009

746.46'041--dc22

                        2008036549

Printed in China

10 9 8 7 6 5

Dedication

To the quilters around the world whose fascination with Sylvia's Bridal Sampler inspired this book.

Acknowledgments

I am grateful to the wonderful quilting friends who contributed blocks to the original Sylvia's Bridal Sampler: Theresa Acker, Barbara Alberti, Mary Althaus, Doris Ast, Sandy Bandt-Coles, Michelle Banton, Beverly Beyer, Adelle P. Bilzing, Carol Bremigan, Therese Bridwell, Jan Browning, Janet L. Carruthers, Ellen Corning, Betsy Crosswaite, Bertie Lou Davis, Mari Y. de Moya, Terry Dorman, Diane Firari, Jonne Fleming, Jeanette Franklin, Diane J. Frauchiger, Sally M. Graff, Sue Hale, Maxine Hameister, Donna R. Johnsen, Sue Johnson, Susie Klostermann, Elinor Koepcke, Carol Donis Krein, Nancy Dunn Kurr, Becki Kurtz, Dianne L. Larson, Linda Lazic, Diane Liebenthal, Nancy Linz, Judith Litman, Rita Loper, Karen Mackowski, Nancy Martin, Mary B. Meier, Alli Mielcarek, Flo Mielcarek, Janet C. Miller, Sharon Miller, Clare Nordman, Suzanne Myers Otto, Isabel Pentony, Terri Petasek, Patty Pohlman, Carol M. Preuss, Sharon Raimondo, Leslie Rector, Betsey Rewey, Rosemary Riederer, Wendy Robertson, Marion Schey, Gail Schlise, Rosemary Schmidt, Nancy Schrader, Cindy Schramm, Pamela Schuster, Pam Skaar, Caraline Smith, Suad Stratton, Joan Stuesser, Annette Tallard, Renee Hoffmann Thompson, Sue Trepte, Ann Tulip, Carol A. Valenta, Sue Vollbrecht, Carol Walters, and Judith H. Ward.

I offer a special thank-you to the quilters who contributed photographs of their beautiful Sylvia's Bridal Samplers: Tanya Anderson, Trisha Chubbs, Simone de Haan, Cobie de Haas, Elise Fare, Barbara Jennekens-Nellestein, Valérie Langue, Susy Parrett, Anne Ida Røkeness, Joan Sheridan, Annelies van den Bergh, and Caroline Van Maele-Delbrouck.

This book would not have been possible without the contributions of the wonderful creative team at C&T Publishing, especially Teresa Stroin, Gailen Runge, Christina Jarumay, Amy Marson, and Kirstie Pettersen. Many thanks to you all.

Contents

How to Find Each Block in the Quilt

We've given you an easy way to find any block within the quilt. The blocks are all coded with a letter for the row and a number for the column that the block is in (see diagram on page 79). For example, Anvil (page 15) is coded as Block I–4. If you go down to Row I and over to Column 4, you will find the Anvil block. If you want to create a quilt exactly like Sylvia's, place your blocks according to their grid numbers.

Introduction

Before it became an international quilting phenomenon, Sylvia's Bridal Sampler began within a story. The novel *The Master Quilter,* to be precise.

In the sixth book in my Elm Creek Quilts series, the staff of a fictional quilters' retreat in picturesque central Pennsylvania conspire to create an extraordinary sampler quilt to celebrate the wedding of founder Sylvia Bergstrom Compson to her beloved Andrew. Sarah, Summer, and the other Elm Creek Quilters spread the word, asking Sylvia's friends, family, and former students to contribute 6″ × 6″ blocks expressing what Sylvia means to each of them as a quilter, teacher, or friend. Blocks soon began arriving from across the country and around the world, accompanied by heartfelt letters expressing abiding friendship and admiration for the renowned Master Quilter. After twists and turns of the plot, in which the blocks are lost and then recovered, Sylvia's friends present her with a beautiful quilt that celebrates the joy of her marriage, as well as the enduring bonds of friendship.

I always enjoy making the quilts featured in my novels so that I can display them on my book tours and on my website. As I awaited the publication of *The Master Quilter,* I followed the Elm Creek Quilters' example and enlisted the help of 72 talented quilting friends from across the country. Supplied with drawings of the blocks and fat eighths from my first fabric line—Sylvia's Collection from Red Rooster Fabrics—my helpers eagerly took to the task. Before long, I had collected 140 lovingly sewn blocks, each bearing the unique tastes of its maker and enhanced by Sue Vollbrecht's beautiful longarm quilting.

Wherever I displayed Sylvia's Bridal Sampler, readers and quilters alike admired it, and many remarked that they would like to make one of their own. To get them started, I included patterns for five of the blocks in my second pattern book, *Return to Elm Creek.* But soon after that book was published, quilters began requesting the remaining 135 blocks, which could not be included in the book due to space limitations.

How could I honor these many requests as quickly as possible? Because so many of the requests for patterns had come via email, the Internet seemed the best solution. So in June 2005, I created a Sylvia's Bridal Sampler website, including a blog in which I posted a new block pattern

every few days. To my delight, quilters began sending in photos of the blocks they had made; with their permission, I posted those photos in a website gallery for other quilters to admire. As the number of Sylvia's Bridal Sampler quilters steadily grew, I created a mailing list so they could exchange advice, offer one another encouragement, and proudly announce milestones they had achieved in their SBS journeys.

To help keep everyone motivated, I launched a Block of the Week program in January 2007, which is still going strong under the direction of Debbie Markowitz. Just for fun, we've held block swaps that have strengthened the bonds of friendship among Sylvia's Bridal Sampler quilters from around the world—and have also resulted in beautiful quilts.

The interest in Sylvia's Bridal Sampler sparked by those five patterns in *Return to Elm Creek* has spread beyond my own website to other thriving online communities. Kansas quilter Kathy Tattershall runs an online discussion list amusingly titled The SBS Offline Quilters. "Kathy has kept us motivated to complete our blocks through monthly challenges and has sent out prizes for those of us who complete the challenge," reports Debbie Madigan, the list moderator, who adds that many of the list members have set up online photo albums to display their completed blocks.

Photo by Cobie de Haas

WARM WITH HEARTS,
80¾″ × 98½″, pieced and quilted by Cobie de Haas, 2007, The Netherlands

I KNOW MY FRIENDS ARE STARS,
70″ × 70″, pieced and appliquéd by Susy Parrott, quilted by Jan Chandler,
2008, United Kingdom

Photo by Susy Parrott

Dutch quilter Annelies van den Bergh, an accomplished quilter and one of the most popular members of the Sylvia's Bridal Sampler mailing list, now sponsors her own mailing list for other Dutch quilters who have been inspired to make their own Sylvia's Bridal Samplers. In early 2006, German quilter Heike Jesse discovered the patterns posted on my website and quickly spread the word to her quilting circle, the Quiltfriends. Before long, she launched her own website, where German quilters post images of their Sylvia's Bridal Samplers in progress on virtual design walls and exchange advice and support. In 2007, Paris quilter Estelle Morin launched a mailing list and website for 23 French-speaking aspiring Sylvia's Bridal Sampler quiltmakers. "Since September, we have been having a Block of the Week challenge," Estelle says. "The members of the list take their turns and give a block every Friday, and then we upload our blocks in the appropriate photo albums. Two of our members have been going through difficult times, so we showed them our support by making SBS blocks for them." Sylvia and the Elm Creek Quilters would surely applaud their kindness and compassion.

Another online group is truly international in scope: The Friends of Elm Creek, created by St. Petersburg, Florida, quilter Althea Conger. These quilters, who hail from the United States, Canada, Ireland, Belgium, France, and Australia, enjoy swapping friendship blocks using patterns from Sylvia's Bridal

Sampler. "This has been a really enjoyable experience for all of us," Althea says. "We have posted pictures of ourselves so we can 'see' the friends we 'talk' to on a daily basis. We have really become good friends and are already planning our next Christmas block project."

But not all Sylvia's Bridal Sampler groups meet online. In Melbourne, Australia, quilters gather at Foothills Fabrics and Threads every month for a Sylvia's Bridal Sampler Sit and Sew. "We are a very mixed bunch of ladies working at our own pace," says shop owner Sandra Mclay. "Some of us are romping through the blocks, whilst others like myself are just plodding along. But we are all certainly enjoying ourselves and are building friendships." These friendships are far-ranging, indeed; some quilters visiting Australia from abroad, such as mailing list favorite Anne Ida Røkeness from Norway, have added a visit to Foothills Fabrics to their itineraries so that they could meet other Sylvia's Bridal Sampler quilters they had originally met via the Internet.

Back in the United States, the Maxville Branch Library Second Saturday Quilting Bees meet in Jacksonville, Florida, to work on their Sylvia's Bridal Samplers together. Elise Fare, an employee of the library and an experienced quilter, set up the program when she heard that local aspiring quilters in the area were interested in taking lessons. The Bees are a mix of beginners and more experienced quilters, Elise explains, adding, "The beginners are getting instructions and those with experience teach and assist the beginners." When Elise's quilt is complete, the quilters plan to display it in the library for a time to thank the staff for providing the Bees with a place to meet.

At Tiny Stitches quilt shop in Marietta, Georgia, the members of the Elm Creek Quilts Club meet on the first Sunday afternoon of each month to work on their Sylvia's Bridal Samplers together. They assign four new blocks to accomplish in the weeks ahead, share the blocks they have completed since their last meeting, discuss the Elm Creek Quilts novels, and enjoy refreshments. "We have about ten to twelve ladies working on the Bridal Sampler," says club member Melinda Fulkerson. "Mine is being done in batik scraps and white background. We have 1930s, blue and white, pink and green, completely scrappy, and lots of other combinations."

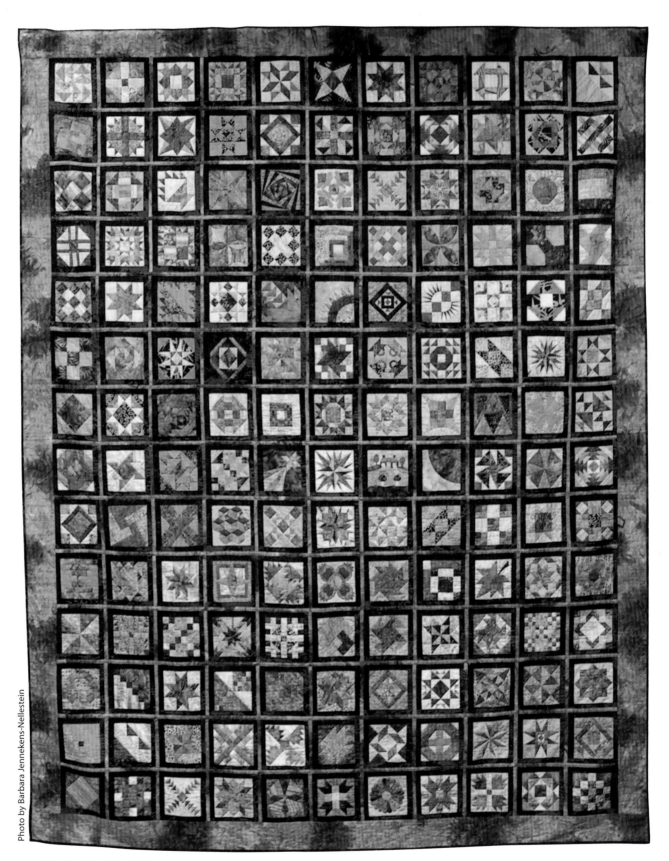

Photo by Barbara Jennekens-Nellestein

SBS DE BONTE STORRUM,
94½˝ × 118˝, pieced, appliquéd and hand-quilted
by Barbara Jennekens-Nellestein, some blocks from Marcia Hohn,
2007, The Netherlands

As enjoyable and rewarding as these virtual and in-person quilting clubs have been, and as much as quilters from around the world have appreciated the resources available on my website, one thing has been missing—something that aspiring Sylvia's Bridal Sampler quilters have requested more than any other—a pattern book. After all, there are limits to what the Internet can offer, and a pattern book would make the task of acquiring the templates and instructions easier and more convenient. Therefore I was delighted when C&T Publishing agreed to make all 140 blocks available, as well as photos of wonderful Sylvia's Bridal Samplers created by quilters from around the world.

If the story of these new Sylvia's Bridal Samplers has captured your imagination the way the original, fictional version did in *The Master Quilter,* I invite you to try your hand at several, many, or all 140 of these pretty blocks, whether you create your own versions of Sylvia's Bridal Sampler or unite them in new combinations to create an exciting original design all your own. However you use these patterns, I hope you will enjoy your journey and share your achievements online at www.sylviasbridalsampler.com. There's always room for more friends in the bridal party!

Photo by Simone de Haan

SIMONE'S BRIDAL QUILT,
78˝ × 101˝, pieced, appliquéd, and quilted by Simone de Haan, 2008, The Netherlands

Photo by Amanda Bolan

INTERNATIONAL SWAP QUILT,
64˝ × 64˝, blocks pieced by 51 people from all over the world, assembled and quilted by Joan Sheridan, 2008, USA

Sylvia's Bridal Sampler
From The Master Quilter

Finished Size: 87" × 115"
Block Size: 6" finished
Number of Blocks: 140
Machine assembled by Jennifer Chiaverini,
machine quilted by Sue Vollbrecht, 2004, USA

The Elm Creek Quilts—Sylvia's Collection fabrics used in this quilt were generously donated by Red Rooster Fabrics.

The 140 different blocks for this quilt were made by my friends and readers. Many thanks to all who helped make this quilt possible!

The Blocks

For detailed information on basic piecing and quilting techniques, please refer to Start Quilting with Alex Anderson, The Art of Classic Quiltmaking *by Harriet Hargrave and Sharyn Craig, or any basic quiltmaking book.*

FABRIC REQUIREMENTS

Note: These figures are approximations only. Yardage amounts will vary depending on your fabric choices in each individual block.

- **Beiges:** 10 yards (includes 2½ yards for the sashing and the inner border)

- **Light roses or reds:** 1½ yards

- **Dark roses or reds:** 1½ yards

- **Light greens:** 2 yards

- **Dark greens:** 2 yards (includes ⅞ yard for the middle border)

- **Medium greens:** 1½ yards

- **Light blues:** 1½ yards

- **Medium blues:** 4¾ yards (includes 2½ yards for the outer border and ⅔ yard for the binding)

- **Dark blues:** 1½ yards

- **Medium tans and browns:** 1½ yards

- **Batting:** 95″ × 123″

- **Backing:** 8⅝ yards

Sylvia & Andrew

Sylvia Bergstrom and Andrew Cooper met in childhood, but it wasn't until they reunited at Elm Creek Manor more than 50 years later that they fell in love and decided to marry. While the Elm Creek Quilters were thrilled that their favorite Master Quilter had discovered new love in her golden years, Andrew's son and daughter were reluctant to see their widowed father remarry. Rather than hold a ceremony his children would not attend, Sylvia and Andrew celebrated a surprise Christmas Eve wedding in the ballroom of Elm Creek Manor, surrounded by their dearest friends.

After enjoying a honeymoon in New York City, Sylvia and Andrew traveled to Andrew's daughter's home in Connecticut, where they announced their big news and took their first steps toward reconciliation. Eventually Andrew's children realized how misguided their objections had been, and they welcomed Sylvia to the family with warmth and affection.

Andrew's children were not the only ones to have been momentarily confounded by Sylvia and Andrew's surprise wedding. Because the Elm Creek Quilters had not expected the couple to marry so soon, they had not sewn even a single stitch for the wedding quilt. Rather than delay presenting the newlyweds with a gift befitting the joyous occasion, the Elm Creek Quilters requested 6-inch blocks from Sylvia's friends, colleagues, and former students, a wonderful variety of blocks that became Sylvia's Bridal Sampler.

In the years to come, Sylvia would often reflect that if she and Andrew had not unexpectedly moved up the date of their wedding, Sylvia's Bridal Sampler never would have been created.

(Block L-3)

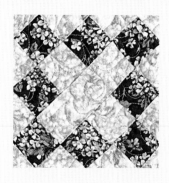

(Block F-6)

Template pattern is on page 85.

1. Cut 2 strips 1½″ × 16″—one from background fabric and the other from green. Place the strips together, right sides facing, and sew along the longest edge. Press toward the green fabric.

2. With a rotary cutter, cross cut 10 strips 1½″ wide from the strip set. Join the strips in pairs, right sides and opposite colors facing, and sew together along the long edge to make 5 four-patches. Press.

3. From brown fabric, cut 4 rectangles 1⅝″ × 3¼″. Cut 2 of the rectangles in half once from the lower left corner to the upper right corner to make 4 B triangles. Cut the remaining 2 rectangles in half once from the lower right corner to the upper left corner to make 4 mirror-image B reverse (Br) triangles.

4. Make 4 triangles from background fabric using template pattern A.

5. Sew 1 B triangle and 1 Br triangle to each A triangle. Press.

6. Sew the block segments into 3 rows as shown. Press. Sew the rows together. Press.

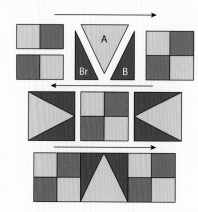

Template patterns are on page 84.

1. Cut 8 squares from red fabric using template pattern A. Cut 2 squares from background fabric using template pattern A.

2. Cut 2 squares 3¼″ × 3¼″ from background fabric. Cut each square diagonally twice to make 8 B triangles.

3. Cut 2 squares 1⅞″ × 1⅞″ from background fabric. Cut each square diagonally once to make 4 C triangles.

4. Cut 1 rectangle from background fabric using template D.

5. Sew the pieces into diagonal rows as shown. Press. Sew the rows together. Press.

(Block C-3)

2. Sew the foundations together. Press.

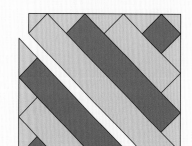

Foundation patterns are on page 84.

1. Make 1 of foundation paper piecing pattern A. Press. Make 1 of foundation paper piecing pattern B. Press.

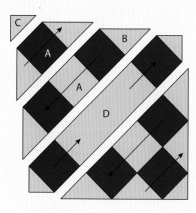

AMETHYST

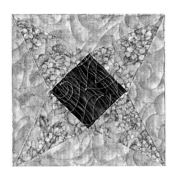

Option 1:
Traditional Piecing

Template patterns are on page 85.

1. From background fabric, make 4 of template pattern C. From light blue fabric, make 4 of template pattern B. From dark blue fabric, make 1 of template pattern A.

2. Join the block pieces into 3 rows as shown. Press.

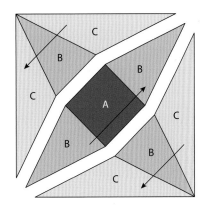

3. Using Y-seam construction, join the rows. Sew from point to point only. Do not sew into the seam allowances. Press.

Option 2:
Foundation Paper Piecing

Foundation pattern is on page 85.

1. Make 4 of the Amethyst foundation pattern. Press.

2. Arrange the foundations as shown and sew into 2 rows. Press. Sew the rows together. Press.

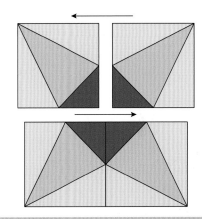

ANVIL

Template patterns are on page 86.

1. From brown fabric, make 2 of template A and 2 of template B.

2. From background fabric, cut 1 square 3⅞″ × 3⅞″. Cut the square in half diagonally once to make 2 large background C triangles.

3. From background fabric, cut 4 squares 2⅜″ × 2⅜″. Cut each square in half diagonally once to make 8 small background D triangles.

4. Sew 2 small background D triangles to each A trapezoid and 2 to each B trapezoid. Press.

5. Sew a large background C triangle to each A trapezoid unit. Press.

6. Sew each A unit from Step 5 to a B unit from Step 4 to make 2 block halves. Press.

7. Sew the block halves together. Press.

◆ ARIZONA

1. From background fabric, cut 4 A squares 1½″ × 1½″.

2. From background fabric, cut 4 B rectangles 1½″ × 2½″.

3. From background fabric, cut 6 squares 1⅞″ × 1⅞″. Cut each square in half once diagonally to make 12 small background C triangles.

4. From red fabric, cut 10 squares 1⅞″ × 1⅞″. Cut each square in half once diagonally to make 20 small red D triangles. Pair each light C triangle with a dark D triangle and sew together along the longest edge to make 12 triangle-squares. Press.

5. From background fabric, cut 1 square 3¼″ × 3¼″. Cut the square in half twice diagonally to make 4 large background F triangles. Take the remaining small red D triangles and sew 2 to each large background F triangle to make 4 Flying Geese units. Press.

6. Cut 1 E square 2½″ × 2½″ from red fabric. Sew 2 background B rectangles to opposite sides of the red E square. Press. Sew 2 Flying Geese to the back-ground rectangles to complete the center row. Press.

7. Arrange the remaining squares and triangle-squares as shown and sew into rows. Press. Sew the rows together. Press.

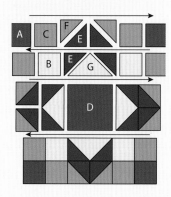

◆ AUNT SUKEY'S CHOICE

1. Cut 4 A squares 1½″ × 1½″ from dark blue, 4 B squares 1½″ × 1½″ from background fabric, and 8 C squares 1½″ × 1½″ from light green. Cut 1 D square 2½″ × 2½″ from brown.

2. Cut 4 squares 1⅞″ × 1⅞″ from light green and 4 squares 1⅞″ × 1⅞″ from dark green. Cut each square once diagonally to make 8 dark green E triangles and 8 light green F triangles. Pair each dark green E triangle with a light green F triangle, right sides together, and sew along the longest edge to make 8 triangle-squares. Press.

3. Cut 4 squares 1⅞″ × 1⅞″ from dark green. Cut each square once diagonally to make 8 dark green triangles. Cut 1 square 3¼″ × 3¼″ from background fabric. Cut the background square twice diagonally to make 4 background G triangles. Pair each background G triangle with 2 dark green E triangles, right sides together, and sew to make 4 Flying Geese units. Press.

4. Sew the E/G Flying Geese, E/F triangle-squares, and A, B, C, and D squares into five rows as shown. Press. Sew the rows together. Press.

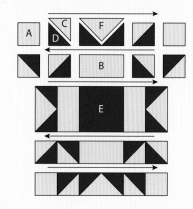

AUTUMN LEAF

Template patterns are on pages 86 and 87.

1. From background fabric, cut 2 rectangles using template A, 6 small triangles using template B, 1 large triangle using template C, 1 large triangle using the reverse of template C (Cr), and 1 square using template D.

2. From dark green, cut 1 trapezoid using template E, 2 trapezoids using template F, 3 trapezoids using the reverse of template F (Fr), and 1 kite using template G.

3. Sew 1 small background B triangle to each E, F, and Fr. Press. Pair each Fr unit with an F unit and sew together as shown. Press. (You will have 1 Fr unit left over.)

4. As shown, sew a background A rectangle to each F/Fr pair: one A to the F side of one pair and the other A to the Fr side of the other pair. Press.

5. Sew the C and Cr triangles to the dark green kite G. Press. Add an A/F/Fr unit to complete the top row as shown. Press.

6. Using your favorite appliqué method, prepare a stem from brown fabric using template H. Appliqué the stem onto the D square. (Note: You may leave the end of the stem as a raw edge where it joins the leaf. It will be hidden within the seam allowance when the separate units are sewn together.)

7. Sew the remaining Fr/B unit to the stem square. Press. Add the E/B unit as shown. Press.

8. To make the bottom row, sew the remaining F/F/A unit to the unit created in Step 7. Press. Sew the 2 rows together. Press.

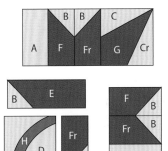

BACHELOR'S PUZZLE

Template pattern is on page 87.

1. From blue fabric, cut 4 pieces using the reverse of template A (Ar). From green fabric, cut 4 pieces using template A.

2. Pair the green A's with the blue Ar's, right sides together, and sew along the longest edge, sewing only from point to point. Do not sew into the seam allowance at either end. Press.

3. From red fabric, cut 4 B squares 2″ × 2″.

4. Set the red B squares into the angles between the green and blue A's. Press.

5. Cut 2 squares 2⅜″ × 2⅜″ from background fabric. Cut each square once along the diagonal to create 4 C triangles.

6. Sew 1 C triangle to each A/Ar/B unit as shown. Press.

7. Cut 1 D square 2⅝″ × 2⅝″ from background fabric.

8. Sew 2 of the units created in Step 6 to opposite sides of the D square. Press. Using Y-seam construction, attach the remaining 2 units, sewing the seams in the order shown. Sew only from point to point, not into the seam allowances. Press.

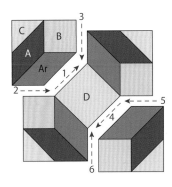

BARRISTER'S BLOCK

(Block K-9)

1. From background fabric, cut:

- 4 A squares 1¼″ × 1¼″.

- 2 squares 3⅛″ × 3⅛″. Cut each square in half diagonally once to make 4 large background B triangles.

- 12 squares 1⅝″ × 1⅝″. Cut each square in half diagonally once to make 24 small background C triangles.

2. From green fabric, cut:

- 2 squares 3⅛″ × 3⅛″. Cut each square in half diagonally once to make 4 large green D triangles.

- 12 squares 1⅝″ × 1⅝″. Cut each square in half diagonally once to make 24 small green E triangles.

3. Pair each large green D triangle with a large background B triangle, right sides together, and sew along the longest edge to make 4 large triangle-squares. Press. Repeat with the small triangles to make 24 small triangle-squares.

4. Sew together 3 small triangle-squares from Step 3 to make a row. Press. Repeat to make a total of 4. Sew together the remaining triangle-squares in groups of 3 to make 4 mirror-image rows. Press.

5. As shown, sew 1 triangle-square row to the green half of 1 large triangle-square. Press. Repeat with the 3 remaining identical triangle-square rows.

6. Sew the small background A squares to the green ends of the mirror-image triangle-square rows. Press.

7. Sew each mirror-image row from Step 6 to a large triangle-square unit from Step 5 to make 4 block quarters. Press.

8. Sew the block quarters into 2 rows as shown. Press. Sew the rows together. Press.

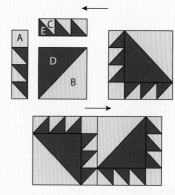

BEAR'S PAW

(Block G-3)

1. Make 4 of foundation paper piecing pattern A. Press. Make 4 of foundation paper piecing pattern B. Press. Pair each A foundation with a B foundation and sew together. Press.

2. Make 4 rectangles from background fabric using template C. Make 1 square from blue using template D.

3. Sew the A/B foundation units, C rectangles, and D square into 3 rows as shown. Sew the 3 rows together. Press.

Template and foundation patterns are on page 87.

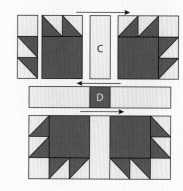

Big T

(Block F-7)

1. Make 2 of foundation paper piecing pattern A for the top and bottom rows. Press. Make 1 each of foundation paper piecing patterns B and C. Press.

2. Sew the B foundation to the C foundation to make the center row. Press.

3. Sew the 3 rows together as shown. Press.

Foundation patterns are on page 88.

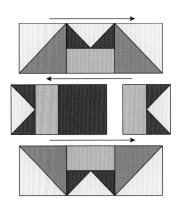

Birds in the Air

(Block I-8)

1. From background fabric, cut 3 squares $2\frac{7}{8}'' \times 2\frac{7}{8}''$. Cut each square in half once diagonally to make 6 background A triangles.

2. From green fabric, cut 1 square $2\frac{7}{8}'' \times 2\frac{7}{8}''$ and cut in half once diagonally to make 2 green B triangles. (You will use only 1 of these triangles for this block; the other may be set aside.) Repeat using blue and brown fabrics.

3. Sew 1 background A triangle to each B triangle to make 3 triangle-squares. Press.

4. Sew 2 triangle-squares together and attach a background triangle as shown. Press.

5. Sew the remaining 2 background triangles to the third triangle-square as shown. Press.

6. Sew the units created in Steps 4 and 5 together. Press.

7. From green fabric, cut 1 square $6\frac{7}{8}'' \times 6\frac{7}{8}''$ and cut in half once diagonally to make 2 green C triangles. (You will use only 1 of these triangles for this block; the other may be set aside.) Sew the green C triangle to the pieced triangle created in Step 6 as shown. Press.

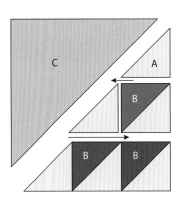

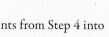

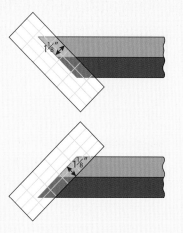

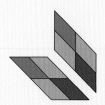

Template patterns are on pages 88 and 89.

1. From dark green, cut 1 strip 1⅛″ × 18″. From blue, cut 1 strip 1⅛″ × 18″. From light green, cut 2 strips 1⅛″ × 18″.

2. Pair the dark green strip with a light green strip, right sides together, and sew along the longest edge. Press the seam toward the dark fabric. With a rotary cutter, trim off one end of the strip pair at a 45° angle. Cut 4 strips 1⅛″ wide at **45°** this angle. Cut 4 more 1⅛″ wide strips at the opposite 45° angle, as shown.

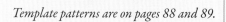

3. Repeat Step 2 with the blue strip and the remaining light green strip. Press the seam toward the blue fabric.

4. Pair each blue/light green strip with a light green/dark green strip, right sides together, and sew to make 8 star points. Press.

5. Join the star points from Step 4 into 4 pairs. Sew from point to point. Do not sew into the seam allowances. Press.

6. From background fabric, cut 4 squares using template A. Set A squares between the star point units from Step 5. Sew from point to point, not into the seam allowances. Press.

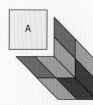

7. Join 2 of the units from Step 6. Press. From background fabric, cut 4 triangles using template B. Using Y-seam construction, set a B triangle between the star points. Press. Repeat to make 2.

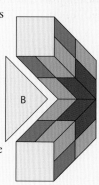

8. Sew the 2 units from Step 7 together. Press. Using Y-seam construction, set the remaining B triangles into the open angles. Press.

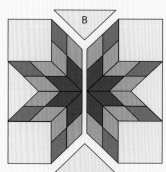

Template patterns are on pages 88 and 89.

1. From dark red, make 1 square using template A.

2. From medium red, make 2 partial squares using template B. From background fabric, make 2 more partial squares using template B.

3. Sewing from point to point only, sew the 2 medium red B partial squares to opposite sides of the A square. Do not sew into the seam allowances. Press.

4. Use Y-seam construction to sew the background fabric B partial squares to opposite sides of the unit from Step 3. Sew the seams in the order shown and do not sew into the seam allowances. Press toward the darker fabrics.

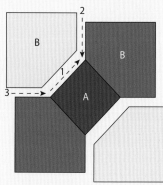

BOY'S NONSENSE

1. Make 2 of foundation paper piecing pattern A. Press. Make 1 of foundation paper piecing pattern B. Press.

2. Sew the A foundations to opposite sides of the B foundation. Press.

Foundation patterns are on page 89.

BRIDE'S BOUQUET

Template patterns are on pages 89 and 90.

1. From light rose fabric, cut 4 diamonds using template A. Join the diamonds in pairs, stitching only from point to point and not into the seam allowance. Press.

2. From dark rose fabric, cut 5 squares using template C. From background fabric, cut 4 triangles using template D. Sew 2 background D triangles to each dark rose C square. Press. Set each D/C/D triangle into a light rose diamond pair. Press.

3. From background fabric, make 3 trapezoids using template B. Flip over the template and make 3 B reverses (Br). Stitching from point to point, sew 1 background trapezoid B to a dark rose C square. Press. Using Y-seam construction, attach a Br trapezoid to the B/C unit. Press. Make 3.

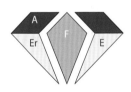

4. Sew the 2 A/C/D units from Step 2 together, stitching from point to point. Press. Using Y-seam construction, attach a B/C/Br unit from Step 3 between the light rose diamonds. Press. Attach the remaining B/C/Br units on opposite ends. Press.

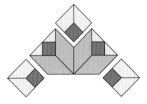

5. From medium green fabric, make 1 kite using template F. From dark green fabric, cut 2 diamonds using template A. From background fabric, cut 1 triangle using template E. Flip over the template and make 1 E reverse (Er) triangle.

6. Attach 1 dark green diamond A to the background triangle E and 1 dark green diamond A to the background triangle Er. Press both. Using Y-seam construction, attach both A/E units to the bouquet stem F. Press.

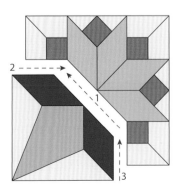

7. Using set-in seam construction, attach the bouquet stem unit to the bouquet flowers unit, sewing the seams in the order shown. Press.

BRIGHT HOPES

1. Make 1 of the Bright Hopes foundation pattern. Press.

Foundation pattern is on page 91.

BROKEN DISHES

1. From background fabric, cut 8 squares 2⅜″ × 2⅜″. From green fabric, cut 8 squares 2⅜″ × 2⅜″.

2. Make 16 green and background fabric quick-pieced triangle-square units:

a. Draw a diagonal line from corner to corner on the wrong side of each background square.

b. Pair a background square with a green square, right sides together. Sew with a ¼″ seam allowance on both sides of the drawn line.

c. Cut on the drawn line to make 2 green/background triangle-squares. Press.

d. Repeat with the remaining background squares and green squares to make a total of 16 triangle-squares.

Sew.
Sew. Cut.

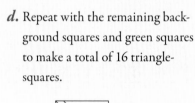

3. Join the green triangle-squares into 4 rows as shown. Press. Sew the rows together. Press.

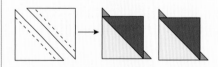

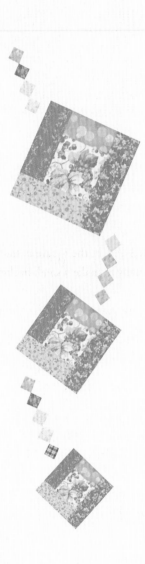

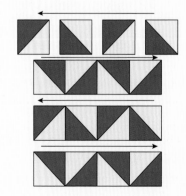

1. From background fabric, cut 2 squares 2⅞″ × 2⅞″. Cut each square in half once diagonally to make 4 large background A triangles. Repeat with 1 square each of focus fabrics: dark red, light red, medium green, and blue.

2. From background fabric, cut 1 square 3¼″ × 3¼″. Cut the square in half twice diagonally to make 4 small background B triangles. Repeat with dark red, light red, medium green, and blue fabrics. (You will use only 2 triangles from each focus fabric. This quick-cutting technique is used to make sure the triangles lie on the proper grain.)

3. Sew 1 small background B triangle to a small dark red B triangle to make a dark red/background B/B triangle pair. Press. Repeat with 3 more small background triangles and 1 each of the remaining focus fabric colors.

4. Sew the blue/background B/B triangle pair to a large light red A triangle. Sew the dark red/background B/B triangle pair to a large blue A triangle. Sew the medium green/background

B/B triangle pair to a large dark red A triangle. Sew the light red/background B/B triangle pair to a large medium green A triangle.

5. Sew 1 large background A triangle to a large light red A triangle to make a triangle-square. Press. Repeat with 3 additional large background A triangles and a large dark red A triangle, a large blue A triangle, and a large medium green A triangle to make triangle-squares in all the focus fabric colors.

6. Sew together 1 small B triangle of each focus fabric color to make a quarter-square triangle unit. Press.

7. Sew the block units into 3 rows as shown. Press. Sew the rows together. Press.

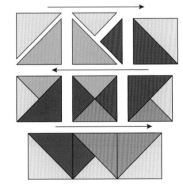

(Block A-7)

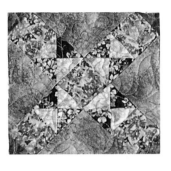

Template pattern is on page 90.

1. From light brown fabric, cut 1 square 5¼″ × 5¼″. Cut the square twice along the diagonals to make 4 A triangles.

2. Cut 2 blue squares 1⅞″ × 1⅞″. Cut each along the diagonal once to make 4 blue B triangles.

3. Cut 4 red squares 1⅞″ × 1⅞″. Cut each along the diagonal once to make 8 red B triangles.

4. Cut 4 background squares 1⅞″ × 1⅞″. Cut each along the diagonal once to make 8 background B triangles.

5. Cut 5 green squares using template C.

6. Join 2 red B triangles and 2 background B triangles to make a 4-triangle unit. Press. Repeat to make 4.

7. Join the C squares, A triangles, blue B triangles, and the 4-triangle units from Step 6 to form 3 rows as shown. Press.

8. Join the rows. Press.

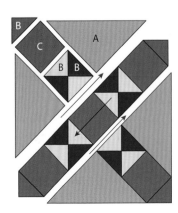

(Block N-2)

(Block E-3)

Template and foundation patterns are on page 90.

1. Make 2 of foundation paper piecing pattern A. Press. Make 2 of foundation paper piecing pattern B. Press.

2. Using template C, make 4 background squares, 4 brown squares, and 1 blue square. Arrange the squares into a nine-patch: Sew the squares into 3 rows, press, and sew the rows together. Press.

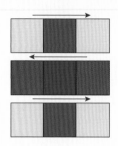

3. Attach the A foundations to opposite sides of the nine-patch. Press.

4. Attach the B foundations to opposite sides of the unit from Step 3. Press.

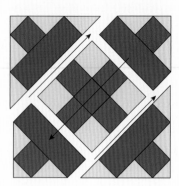

⊞ CHILDREN'S DELIGHT

(Block B-4)

1. Cut 4 dark blue squares 1¾″ × 1¾″. Cut 1 background square 1¾″ × 1¾″.

2. Cut 1 dark blue square 2¾″ × 2¾″.

3. Cut 4 background rectangles 1¾″ × 2¾″.

4. Cut 2 blue rectangles 1¾″ × 5¼″.

5. Sew the nine-patch first. Press. Attach a blue rectangle to one side. Press.

6. Sew the background square to the remaining blue rectangle. Press. Sew this row to the unit created in Step 5. Press.

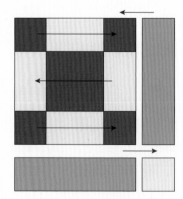

CHIMNEYS AND CORNERSTONES

(Block G-4)

1. Cut 6 squares 1½″ × 1½″ from red. Cut 1 square 1½″ × 1½″ from background fabric and 1 from any dark fabric except red.

2. Sew 1 red square to a background square. Press. Sew 1 red square to the dark square. Press. Sew the square pairs together to make a four-patch. Press.

3. Cut 1 rectangle 1½″ × 2½″ from background fabric and 1 from a dark fabric. Sew the 2 rectangles to opposite sides of the four-patch unit. Press.

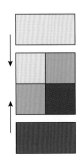

4. From background fabric, cut 1 rectangle 1½″ × 3½″, 1 rectangle 1½″ × 4½″, and 1 rectangle 1½″ × 5½″. From dark fabrics, cut 1 rectangle 1½″ × 3½″, 1 rectangle 1½″ × 4½″, and 1 rectangle 1½″ × 5½″.

5. Sew a red square to 1 end of each of the two 1½″ × 3½″ rectangles and the two 1½″ × 5½″ rectangles, both light and dark. Press.

6. Sew the 1½″ × 3½″ rectangle/red square strips from Step 5 to opposite sides of the unit from Step 3. Press.

7. Sew the 1½″ × 4½″ rectangles to opposite sides of the unit from Step 6. Press.

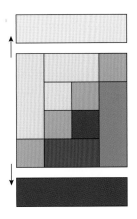

8. Sew the 1½″ × 5½″ rectangle/red square strips from Step 5 to opposite sides of the unit from Step 7. Press.

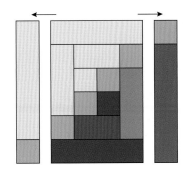

CHINESE COIN

(Block A-9)

1. Cut 2 background squares 3¼″ × 3¼″. Cut each once along the diagonal to make 4 background A triangles.

2. Cut 2 light rose squares 3¼″ × 3¼″. Cut each once along the diagonal to make 4 light rose B triangles.

3. Cut 1 background C squares 1¾″ × 1¾″. *cut 4 background E rectangles 1 3/4 x 1 5/8*

4. Cut 4 dark rose D squares 1¾″ × 1¾″.

5. Pair each background A triangle with a light rose B triangle, right sides together. Sew each pair along the long edge to make 4 triangle-squares. Press.

6. Join squares and triangle-squares to form 3 rows. Press.

7. Join the rows. Press.

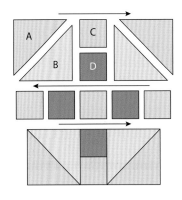

CHURN DASH

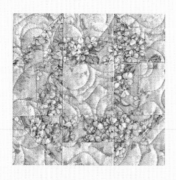

1. From background fabric, cut 1 strip 1½″ × 12″. Cut another 1½″ × 12″ strip from blue. Pair the strips, right sides together, and sew along the longest edge. Press.

2. With a rotary cutter, cut the blue/background strip from Step 1 into 4 blue/background squares 2½″ × 2½″.

3. Cut 4 squares 2⅞″ × 2⅞″ from blue fabric. Cut 4 squares 2⅞″ × 2⅞″ from background fabric.

4. Make 4 quick-pieced triangle-squares (see page 22, Step 2) from the blue and background 2⅞″ × 2⅞″ squares. Press.

5. From background fabric, cut 1 square 2½″ × 2½″.

6. Sew the block segments into 3 rows. Press. Sew the rows together. Press.

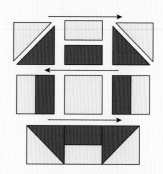

CLAY'S CHOICE

1. From background fabric, cut 4 rectangles 2″ × 3½″ and 2 squares 2⅜″ × 2⅜″.

2. From medium green fabric, cut 2 squares 2⅜″ × 2⅜″. From blue fabric, cut 4 squares 2⅜″ × 2⅜″.

3. Make 4 quick-pieced triangle-squares (see page 22, Step 2) from the blue and background 2⅜″ × 2⅜″ squares. Press.

4. Repeat Step 3 with the medium green squares and the remaining blue squares to make 4 green/blue triangle-squares.

5. Sew each blue/background triangle-square to a green/blue triangle-square as shown. Press. Sew a background rectangle to each pair. Press.

6. Sew the block units into 2 rows. Press. Sew the rows together. Press.

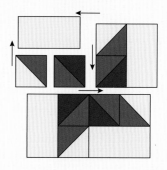

CONTRARY HUSBAND

1. Cut 1 brown A square 3½″ × 3½″.

2. Cut 4 blue squares 2⅜″ × 2⅜″. Cut 4 background squares 2⅜″ × 2⅜″. Cut each square once along the diagonal to make 8 blue B triangles and 8 background C triangles.

3. Cut 4 blue D squares 2″ × 2″.

4. Arrange the pieces as shown. Sew into 3 rows. Press. Sew the rows together. Press.

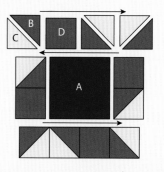

CONTRARY WIFE

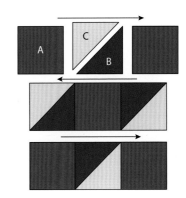

(Block L-10)

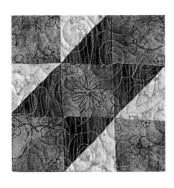

1. From blue fabric, cut 5 A squares 2½″ × 2½″.

2. From medium green fabric, cut 2 squares 2⅞″ × 2⅞″. From background fabric, cut 2 squares 2⅞″ × 2⅞″. Cut each square once along the diagonal to make 4 medium green B triangles and 4 background C triangles.

3. Arrange the pieces as shown. Sew into 3 rows. Press. Sew the rows together. Press.

CORN AND BEANS

(Block E-2)

1. Cut 10 squares 1⅞″ × 1⅞″ from background fabric. Cut each square once diagonally to make 20 triangles.

2. Cut 6 squares 1⅞″ × 1⅞″ from light green fabric. Cut each square once diagonally to make 12 triangles.

3. Pair each light green triangle with a background triangle, right sides together. Sew each pair along the longest edge to make 12 triangle-squares. Press.

4. Sew 1 background triangle to a triangle-square from Step 3. Press. Repeat to make 8.

5. Cut 4 squares 1⅞″ × 1⅞″ from dark green fabric. Cut each square once diagonally to make 8 triangles. Sew 1 dark green triangle to 4 of the units created in Step 4 and to each remaining triangle-square. Press.

6. Arrange the units created in Steps 4 and 5 into 3 offset rows and sew together. Press.

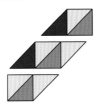

7. Cut 2 squares 2⅞″ × 2⅞″ from light red fabric. Cut each square once diagonally to make 4 triangles. Sew 1 triangle to each unit created in Step 6. Press.

8. Cut 1 square 2⅞″ × 2⅞″ from dark blue. Cut 1 square 2⅞″ × 2⅞″ from light blue. Cut each square diagonally to make 2 dark blue triangles and 2 light blue triangles. Sew a blue triangle to each of the 4 units created in Step 7. Press.

9. Arrange the units created in Step 8 into 2 rows. Press. Sew the rows together. Press.

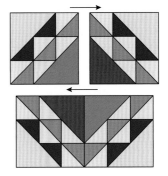

COURTHOUSE STEPS

(Block N-1)

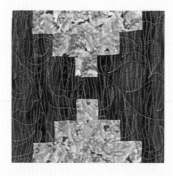

Foundation pattern is on page 92.

1. Make 1 of the Courthouse Steps foundation pattern. Press.

CROSS AND CROWN

(Block B-3)

Template and foundation patterns are on page 91.

1. Make 4 of the foundation paper piecing pattern.

2. Make 4 of template A. Make 1 of template B.

3. Arrange the segments as shown. Sew into 3 rows. Press. Sew the rows together. Press.

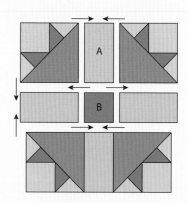

CROSSED CANOES

(Block C-6)

Foundation pattern is on page 93.

1. Make 2 of the foundation paper piecing pattern. Press. Make 2 of the foundation paper piecing pattern in the reverse colors (swap the light colors for dark and vice versa). Press.

2. Sew the foundations into 2 rows as shown. Press. Sew the rows together. Press.

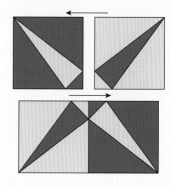

CROWN OF THORNS

(Block G-8)

Foundation patterns are on pages 92 and 93.

1. Make 2 of foundation paper piecing pattern A. Make 2 of foundation paper piecing pattern B. Make 1 of foundation paper piecing pattern C.

2. Sew the B foundations to opposite sides of the C foundation to make the center row. Press.

3. Sew the 2 A foundations to the center row. Press.

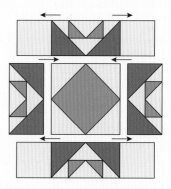

CROW'S FOOT

(Block B-6)

Foundation patterns are on page 93.

1. Make 2 of foundation paper piecing pattern A. Press. Repeat to make 2 of foundation paper piecing pattern B.

2. Pair each A foundation with a B foundation and sew together as shown. Press.

3. Make 2 of foundation paper piecing pattern A using the *reverse* of the colorway made in Step 1. Press. Repeat to make 2 of foundation paper piecing pattern B.

4. Pair each A foundation with a B foundation and sew together as shown. Press.

5. Sew the segments into 2 rows as shown. Press. Sew the rows together. Press.

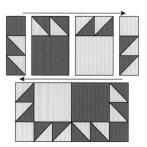

CUT GLASS DISH

(Block N-4)

1. From background fabric, cut 3 squares 2½″ × 2½″ and 12 squares 1⅞″ × 1⅞″. From green fabric, cut 12 squares 1⅞″ × 1⅞″.

2. Make 24 quick-pieced triangle-square units (see page 22, Step 2) from the 1⅞″ × 1⅞″ background and green squares. Press.

3. Sew 4 triangle-squares into a row. Press. Repeat to make 4 rows.

4. Sew the remaining triangle-squares together in pairs. Press. Sew the pairs together to make 2 four-patches. Press.

5. Sew the block units into 3 rows as shown. Press. Sew the rows together. Press.

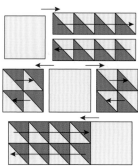

DIAMOND FRIENDSHIP

(Block N-10)

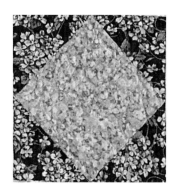

1. From blue fabric, cut 1 square 4¾″ × 4¾″.

2. From red fabric, cut 2 squares 3⅞″ × 3⅞″. Cut each square in half diagonally once to make 4 large red triangles.

3. Sew 2 red triangles to opposite sides of the blue square. Press.

4. Sew the remaining red triangles to the other opposite sides of the blue square. Press.

(**Note:** You can use the blue square to sign your quilt with your name, location, and the date you completed your quilt.)

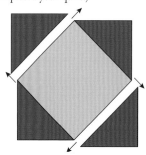

DOGTOOTH VIOLET

(Block M-8)

Foundation patterns are on page 94.

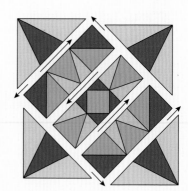

1. Make 2 of foundation paper piecing pattern A, 1 of B, 2 of C, and 4 of D. Press.

2. Sew the 2 C foundations to opposite sides of the B foundation. Press.

3. Sew the 2 A foundations to opposite sides of the C/B/C unit from Step 2. Press.

4. Sew 2 D foundations to opposite sides of the unit from Step 3. Press. Sew the remaining D foundations to the other 2 sides of the unit. Press.

DOUBLE NINE-PATCH

(Block N-8)

Template patterns are on page 93.

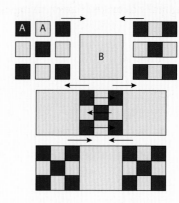

1. From green fabric, cut 25 squares using template A.

2. From background fabric, cut 20 squares using template A and 4 squares using template B.

3. Make 5 nine-patch units. Press.

4. Sew the B squares and nine-patches into 3 rows. Press. Sew the rows together. Press.

(Block H-4)

Template pattern is on page 95.

1. From background fabric, cut 10 squares 1¾″ × 1¾″. Cut each square in half once diagonally to make 20 background triangles.

2. From green fabric, cut 8 squares 1¾″ × 1¾″. Cut each square in half once diagonally to make 16 green triangles.

3. Pair each green triangle with a background triangle to make 16 triangle-squares. Sew the triangle-squares into pairs as shown. Press.

4. Cut 4 squares 1⅜″ × 1⅜″ from green fabric. Sew each square to the end of a triangle-square pair as shown. Press.

5. Make 4 of template A from brown fabric. Sew 1 background triangle to each A. Press.

6. Sew 1 triangle-square pair from Step 3 and 1 triangle-square/square pair from Step 4 to each unit created in Step 5 to make 4 corner units. Press between additions.

7. Cut 4 rectangles 1¼″ × 3⅛″ from blue fabric.

8. Cut 1 square 1¼″ × 1¼″ from green fabric. Sew 2 background rectangles to opposite sides of this square. Press.

9. Sew the units into 3 rows as shown. Sew the rows together. Press.

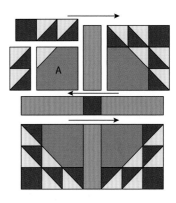

(Block M-3)

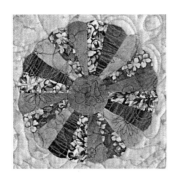

Template patterns are on page 94.

1. Using template A, make 4 wedges from red, 4 from blue, 4 from dark green, 4 from brown, and 4 from medium green.

2. Sew together 1 of each color along the longest edges to make a plate quarter. (It is fine to sew through the seam allowance at the base of the wedge, but stop and backstitch at the

dot where the curve begins at the top of the wedge.) Press. Repeat to make 4.

3. Sew 2 block quarters together to make a block half. Press. Repeat to make the other half. Sew the halves together. Press.

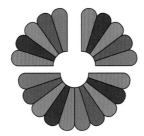

4. Using your favorite appliqué method, make a circle appliqué from medium blue using template B. Appliqué the medium blue circle to the center of the plate.

5. Cut 1 square 6½″ × 6½″ from background fabric. Fold and press vertically, horizontally, and twice diagonally to mark the center of the square.

6. Fold under the seam allowances of the plate, center it on the background square, and appliqué in place. If desired, carefully trim away the extra fabric behind the appliqué.

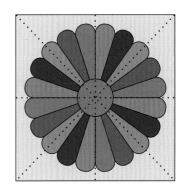

⬛ DUCK AND DUCKLINGS

Template patterns are on page 94.

1. From light red fabric, cut 4 triangles using template A. From dark red fabric, cut 1 square using template B.

2. From green fabric, cut 4 triangles using template C.

3. From background fabric, cut 12 triangles using template A and 4 rectangles using template D.

4. Sew each red A triangle to a background A triangle to make 4 triangle-squares. Press.

5. Sew 2 background A triangles to each triangle-square from Step 4. Press. Sew a green C triangle to each unit to make 4 block corners. Press.

6. Sew 2 block corners to opposite sides of a background D rectangle to make the top row. Press. Repeat to make the bottom row.

7. Sew 2 background D rectangles to opposite sides of the red B square to make the center row. Press.

8. Sew the rows together. Press.

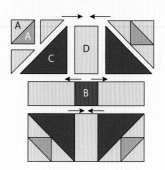

⬛ DUTCHMAN'S PUZZLE

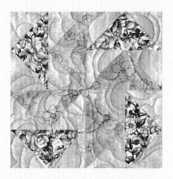

1. From background fabric, cut 8 squares 2⅜″ × 2⅜″. Cut each square in half diagonally once to make 16 background triangles.

2. From red fabric, cut 1 square 4¼″ × 4¼″. Cut in half diagonally twice to make 4 red triangles.

3. From green fabric, cut 1 square 4¼″ × 4¼″. Cut in half diagonally twice to make 4 green triangles.

4. Sew 2 background triangles to each red and green triangle to make 4 red and 4 green Flying Geese. Press toward the background.

5. Sew each green Flying Geese unit to a red Flying Geese unit. Press.

6. Sew the Flying Geese pairs into rows. Press. Sew the rows together. Press.

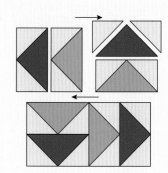

FARMER'S DAUGHTER

(Block J-3)

Template patterns are on page 95.

1. Using template A, make 4 from dark green, 8 from background fabric, and 1 from red. Put aside 4 of the background fabric squares for Step 6. Sew the squares into a nine-patch as shown.

2. Using template B, make 8 triangles from dark green fabric.

3. Using template C, make 4 trapezoids from medium green fabric.

4. Sew 2 dark green B triangles to opposite sides of each C trapezoid. Press.

5. Sew 2 trapezoid units from Step 4 to opposite sides of the nine-patch unit from Step 1 to make the center row. Press.

6. Sew 2 A background squares to opposite sides of the remaining trapezoid units to make the top and bottom rows. Press.

7. Sew the 3 rows together. Press.

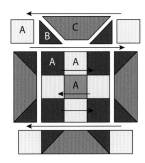

FOLLOW THE LEADER

(Block J-10)

Template patterns are on page 95.

1. Using template A, make 5 squares from brown fabric.

2. Using template B, make 8 small triangles from background fabric.

3. Using template C, make 4 triangles from background fabric and 4 from dark green. Pair dark triangles with light, right sides together, and sew along the longest side. Press.

4. Using template D, make 4 triangles from light green fabric.

5. Sew 2 small background B triangles to each brown A square as shown. Press. Attach a light green D triangle to each to make 4 corner units. Press.

6. Sew 2 C/C units from Step 3 to opposite sides of the background A square to make the center row. Press.

7. Sew 2 corner units from Step 5 to opposite sides of the remaining C/C units to make the top and bottom rows. Press.

8. Sew the 3 rows together. Press.

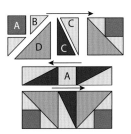

FOOL'S PUZZLE

(Block F-2)

Template patterns are on page 95.

1. Using template A, make 12 arcs from background fabric and 4 arcs from blue.

2. Using template B, make 12 wedges from blue and 4 wedges from background fabric.

3. Matching lights with darks, pair each A arc with a B wedge and sew together. Press.

4. Sew the units into 4 rows as shown. Press. Sew the rows together. Press.

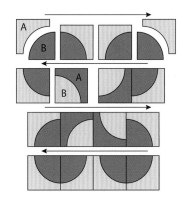

FRIENDSHIP QUILT

(Block L-1)

1. Cut 2 squares 2⅞″ × 2⅞″ from background fabric. Cut each square in half diagonally once to make 4 background triangles. Repeat with blue fabric to make 4 blue triangles.

2. Pair each blue triangle with a background triangle and sew along the longest edge to make 4 triangle-squares.

3. From medium green fabric, cut 2 strips 1³⁄₁₆″ × 12″. (This is an unusual measurement that is necessary because of the block size. Most rulers do not mark to ¹⁄₁₆″, so you will need to judge the midpoint between 1⅛″ and 1¼″.) Cut a third strip 1³⁄₁₆″ × 12″ from red fabric. Sew the 3 strips together, with the red strip in the middle. Press. Your strip set should be 2½″ wide.

4. With your rotary cutter, cut the strip set into four 2½″ × 2½″ squares.

5. Cut 1 square 2½″ × 2½″ from background fabric.

6. Sew the block segments into 3 rows as shown. Press. Sew the rows together. Press.

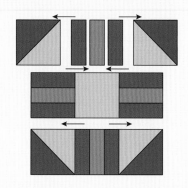

GENTLEMAN'S FANCY

(Block K-6)

Foundation patterns are on page 96.

1. Make 2 of foundation paper piecing pattern A. Press. Make 1 of foundation paper piecing pattern B. Press.

2. Sew the A foundations to opposite sides of the B foundation as shown. Press.

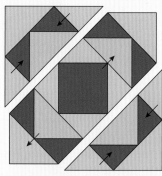

FRIENDSHIP STAR

(Block B-10)

1. Cut 2 green squares 2⅞″ × 2⅞″. Cut 2 background squares 2⅞″ × 2⅞″.

2. Make 4 quick-pieced green/background triangle-squares (see page 22, Step 2). Press.

3. Cut 1 green square 2½″ × 2½″. Cut 4 background squares 2½″ × 2½″.

4. Sew the sections into 3 rows as shown. Press. Sew the 3 rows together. Press.

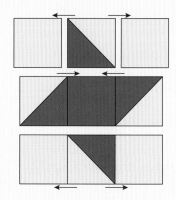

GLORIFIED NINE-PATCH

Option 1: Template Piecing

Template patterns are on pages 96 and 97.

1. From green fabric, cut 4 kites using template A and cut 1 square 1¾″ × 1¾″.

2. From background fabric, make 4 of template B and 4 of template C.

3. Sew 2 green A's to opposite sides of 1 background B to make the top row. Press. Repeat to make the bottom row.

4. Sew the 2 remaining B's to opposite sides of the green square to make the middle row. Press. Sew the 3 rows together to make a nine-patch unit. Press.

5. Sew 2 background C's to opposite sides of the nine-patch. Press. Sew the remaining C's to the other pair of opposite sides. Press.

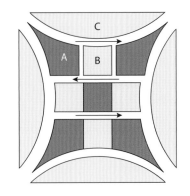

Option 2: Appliqué

Template pattern is on page 97.

1. From green fabric, cut 1 square 1¾″ × 1¾″ and 4 squares 2⅞″ × 2⅞″.

2. From background fabric, cut 4 rectangles 1¾″ × 2⅞″.

3. Following the piecing diagram, sew the rectangles and squares into 3 rows.

Press. Sew the rows together to make an unequal nine-patch. Press.

4. Using your favorite appliqué method, prepare 4 appliqués from background fabric using template D. (Note Template D does *not* include a seam allowance. In addition to any seam allowance your appliqué method adds, leave an extra ½″ along the straight edge to be trimmed later.)

5. Appliqué the 4 background D pieces in place as shown. Press. Carefully trim the block to measure 6½″ × 6½″. If desired, trim away the excess fabric behind the appliqués to reduce bulk.

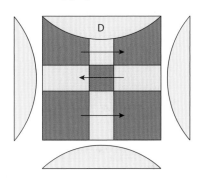

GRACE'S FRIENDSHIP

Template patterns are on page 97.

1. Cut 1 square 8″ × 8″ from light blue for the block background. Referring to the diagram on page 97, lightly mark the placement of the appliqué shapes on the light blue square, centering the design on the square.

2. Cut out and appliqué the shapes, using your favorite method and according to the numerical order on the pattern. (Note: The appliqué shapes do *not* include a seam allowance.)

3. Trim the background block to 6½″ × 6½″. (This includes a ¼″ seam allowance on all sides.)

GRANDMOTHER'S FAN

(Block K-8)

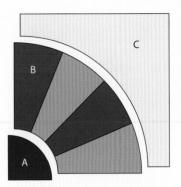

Template patterns are on page 98.

1. Make 1 quarter circle from brown fabric using template A.

2. Make 2 fan segments from green fabric and 2 from red using template B. Sew the B pieces into an arc, alternating colors. Press.

3. Make 1 of template C from background fabric.

4. Sew the pieced arc to the A quarter circle, taking care not to stretch the bias edges. Press.

5. Sew the background C piece to the fan. Press.

GRANDMOTHER'S FLOWER GARDEN

(Block B-5)

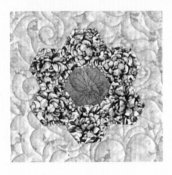

Template pattern is on page 99.

1. Cut 7 of the Grandmother's Flower Garden template from freezer paper.

2. Iron 6 of the freezer-paper templates to the wrong side of medium green fabric and 1 to the wrong side of dark green. Cut out 7 hexagons.

3. Attach 3 medium green hexagons to the dark green hexagon, sewing only from point to point, not into the seam allowances. Press.

4. Using Y-seam construction, attach the remaining medium green hexagons, sewing the seams from point to point (not into the seam allowances) in the order indicated. Press.

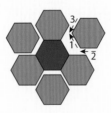

5. Baste under the seam allowance around the outer edges of the 7-hexagon unit.

6. Cut a 6½″ × 6½″ square from background fabric. Find the center by folding it in half vertically, horizontally, and then along both diagonals.

7. Center the 7-hexagon unit on the background square and appliqué in place. Remove the basting. Working from the back of the block, *carefully* trim the extra fabric behind the appliqué and remove the freezer paper.

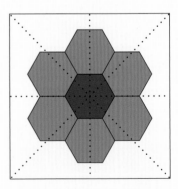

GRANDMOTHER'S PRIDE

Template pattern is on page 98.

1. From light rose, cut 8 A squares. From brown, cut 4 A squares. From background fabric, cut 1 A square.

2. From background fabric, cut 2 squares 3¼″ × 3¼″, then cut diagonally twice to make 8 B triangles.

3. From background fabric, cut 2 squares 1⅞″ × 1⅞″, then cut diagonally once to make 4 C triangles.

4. Sew the pieces into diagonal rows and press.

5. Sew the rows together. Press.

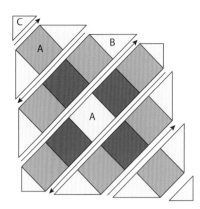

GRAPE BASKET

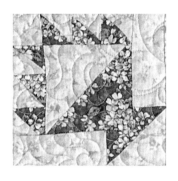

Template patterns are on page 99.

1. Make 8 template A triangles from brown. Make 6 template A triangles from background fabric. Set aside 2 of the brown triangles. Pair the remaining brown triangles with background triangles and sew together along the longest side. Press toward the brown.

2. Sew the triangle-squares made in Step 1 into 2 mirror-image groups of 3 as shown. Press.

3. Make 1 template B square from background fabric and sew it to one of the triangle-square groups as shown. Press.

4. Make 1 template C triangle from brown and 1 from background fabric. Sew them together along the longest side. Press toward the brown.

5. Make 2 template D rectangles from background fabric. Sew 1 brown triangle A to each D rectangle as shown.

6. Sew the 3–triangle-square row from Step 2 to the large triangle-square created in Step 4. Press. Attach the triangle-square/B row from Step 3 as shown. Press.

7. Attach the D/A units created in Step 5 to the unit from Step 6. Press. Make 1 template E triangle from background fabric and sew along the longest edge to complete the last corner. Press.

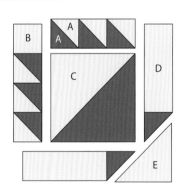

✦ GULF STAR

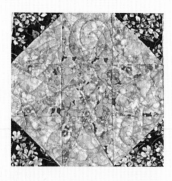

Foundation patterns are on page 98.

1. Make 1 of foundation paper piecing pattern A.

2. Make 4 of foundation paper piecing pattern B.

3. Cut 2 squares 2⅞″ × 2⅞″ from red fabric. Cut each square once on the diagonal to make 4 C triangles. Repeat with the light red fabric.

4. Pair each red triangle with a light red triangle. Sew together along the longest edge. Press.

5. Sew the segments into 3 rows as shown. Press. Sew the rows together. Press.

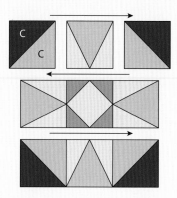

✦ HANDS ALL AROUND

Template patterns are on pages 98 and 99.

1. From brown fabric, cut 8 diamonds using template A. From green, cut 8 diamonds using template A. From background fabric, cut 8 triangles using template B and cut 8 squares using template C. From light red, cut 1 center shape using template D. From blue, cut 4 wedges using template E.

2. Sew a brown and a green A diamond together, sewing only from point to point and not into the seam allowances. Press. Using Y-seam construction, set a B background triangle into the angle. Press. Repeat to make 8 A/B units.

3. Sew together 2 A/B units from Step 2, sewing only from point to point and not into the seam allowances. Press. Using Y-seam construction, set a C background square into the angle. Press. Repeat to create 4 A/B/C units.

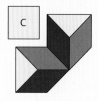

4. Sew the 4 E wedges to the central D. Press.

5. Sew the remaining C squares to the E wedges, sewing only from point to point and not into the seam allowances. Press.

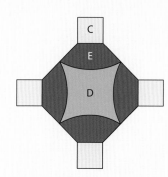

6. Sewing the seams in the order shown, attach 2 A/B/C units from Step 3 to opposite sides of the central unit and adjacent C squares. Press. Attach the remaining 2 A/B/C units. Press.

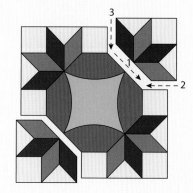

HANDY ANDY

1. Make 1 of foundation paper piecing pattern A, 2 of B, 2 of C, and 2 of D. Press.

2. Sew the 2 B foundations to the A foundation. Press.

3. Sew the C foundations to opposite sides of the B/A/B square. Press.

4. Attach the 2 D foundations. Press.

Foundation patterns are on page 100.

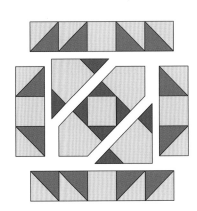

HUNTER'S STAR

1. Make 4 of foundation paper piecing pattern A. Make 4 of foundation paper piecing pattern B. Press.

2. Pair each A foundation with a B foundation and sew together along the longest edge. Press.

3. Sew the units into 2 rows as shown. Press. Sew the rows together. Press.

Foundation patterns are on page 101.

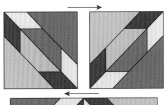

INDIANA ROSE

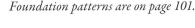

Template patterns are on page 101.

1. Using your favorite appliqué method, prepare 4 roses from medium red using template A, 4 stems from green using template B, 1 small flower from medium blue using template C, and 1 flower center from dark blue using template D. (Note The appliqué shapes do *not* include a seam allowance.)

2. Cut 1 square 8″ × 8″ from background fabric.

3. Fold the square in half vertically, horizontally, and diagonally both ways, pressing after each fold to create placement lines.

4. Following the placement diagram on page 101, appliqué the pieces to the background square in alphabetical order: A-roses, B-stems, C-small flower, D-flower center. (If you wish, you can appliqué the D center to the C flower before appliquéing to the background square.) You do not need to appliqué the raw edges covered by other appliqués, but you may want to baste them. Note the overlaps shown in the upper left quadrant of the pattern.

5. Press and trim the square to 6½″ × 6½″.

IRISH CHAIN

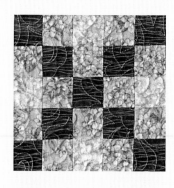

(Block B-9)

- Dark blue, light blue, background, light blue, dark blue: Make 2.

- Light blue, dark blue, light blue, dark blue, light blue: Make 2.

- Background, light blue, dark blue, light blue, background: Make 1.

2. Sew the rows together as shown. Press.

Option 1: Foundation Paper Piecing

Foundation pattern is on page 100.

1. Make 5 rows using the foundation paper piecing pattern and using the following color placement:

Option 2: Template Piecing

Template pattern is on page 101.

1. From dark blue, cut 9 squares using the template. From light blue, cut 12 squares. From background fabric, cut 4 squares.

2. Sew the squares into rows as shown. Press. Sew the rows together. Press.

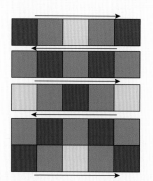

JACK IN THE BOX

(Block M-4)

1. Make 2 of foundation paper piecing pattern A. Make 2 of foundation paper piecing pattern B. Make 1 of foundation paper piecing pattern C. Press all.

2. Sew each A foundation to a B foundation to make the top and bottom rows. Press.

3. Sew the A/B foundations to opposite sides of the C foundation as shown. Press.

Foundation patterns are on page 102.

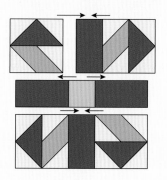

JACK IN THE PULPIT

(Block E-6)

1. Make 1 of foundation paper piecing pattern A. Make 4 of foundation paper piecing pattern B. Press all.

2. Attach 2 B foundations to opposite sides of the A foundation. Press.

3. Sew the remaining 2 B foundations to the remaining sides of the A foundation. Press.

Foundation patterns are on page 103.

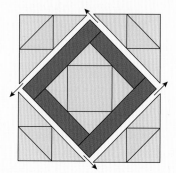

JACOB'S LADDER

1. From background fabric, cut 2 squares 2⅞″ × 2⅞″. From dark green, cut 2 squares 2⅞″ × 2⅞″.

2. Make 4 quick-pieced dark green/background triangle-squares (see page 22, Step 2). Press.

3. From dark blue fabric, cut 1 strip 16″ × 1½″. Repeat with light blue fabric. Pair light and dark strips, right sides facing, and sew together along the longest edge. Press toward the darker fabric. Using a rotary cutter, cut 10 strips 1½″ wide.

4. Sew the strips together in pairs with seams abutted and alternate colors facing. Make 5 four-patches. Press.

5. Sew the block segments into 3 rows as shown. Press. Sew the rows together. Press.

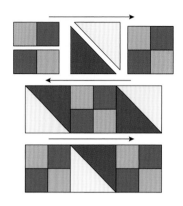

KALEIDOSCOPE

Template pattern is on page 102.

1. From background fabric, cut 2 squares 2⅝″ × 2⅝″. Cut each square in half diagonally once to make 4 background B triangles.

2. Using template A, make 4 triangles from dark red fabric and 4 from light red fabric.

3. Sew 1 B background triangle to each dark red A triangle. Press.

4. Sew a light red triangle to each unit created in Step 3. Press.

5. Sew the units from Step 4 into pairs to make 2 block halves. Press.

6. Sew the block halves together. Press.

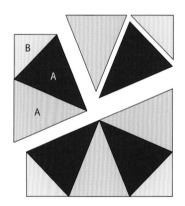

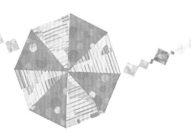

1. From background fabric, cut:

- 4 squares 1¼" × 1¼".

- 10 squares 1⅝" × 1⅝".
  Cut each square in half diagonally once to make 20 small background triangles.

2. From dark blue fabric, cut:

- 2 squares 3⅛" × 3⅛".
  Cut each square in half diagonally once to make 4 large dark blue triangles.

- 12 squares 1⅝" × 1⅝".
  Cut each square in half diagonally once to make 24 small dark blue triangles.

3. From light blue fabric, cut:

- 2 squares 1⅝" x 1⅝".
  Cut each square in half diagonally once to make 4 small light blue triangles.

- 2 squares 3⅛" x 3⅛".
  Cut each square in half diagonally once to make 4 large light blue triangles.

4. Pair each large dark blue triangle with a large light blue triangle, right sides together, and sew along the longest edge to make 4 large triangle-squares. Press. Repeat with the small dark blue triangles to make 20 small dark blue/background triangle-squares and 4 small dark blue/light blue triangle-squares. Press.

5. Sew 3 small dark blue/background triangle-squares together to make a row. Press. Repeat to make a total of 4. Sew the remaining dark blue/background triangle-squares together in pairs and attach a dark blue/light blue triangle-square to each to make 4 mirror-image rows. Press.

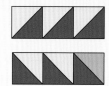

6. Sew 1 dark blue/light blue row to the dark blue half of 1 large triangle-square. Repeat with the 3 remaining identical dark blue/light blue rows. Press.

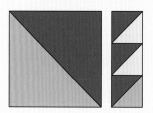

7. Sew the small background squares to the blue ends of the all-blue triangle-square rows. Sew each of these rows to a unit from Step 6 to make 4 block quarters.

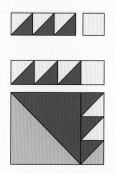

8. Sew the block quarters into 2 rows as shown. Press. Sew the rows together. Press.

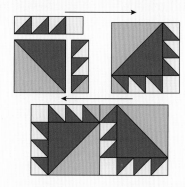

Key West Beauty

(Block M-10)

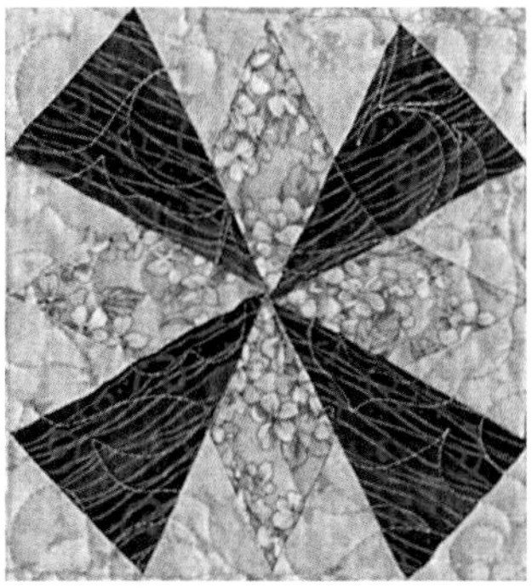

Foundation pattern is on page 103.

1. Make 4 of foundation paper piecing pattern A. Press.

2. Sew the foundations into pairs to make 2 block halves. Press. Sew the halves together. Press.

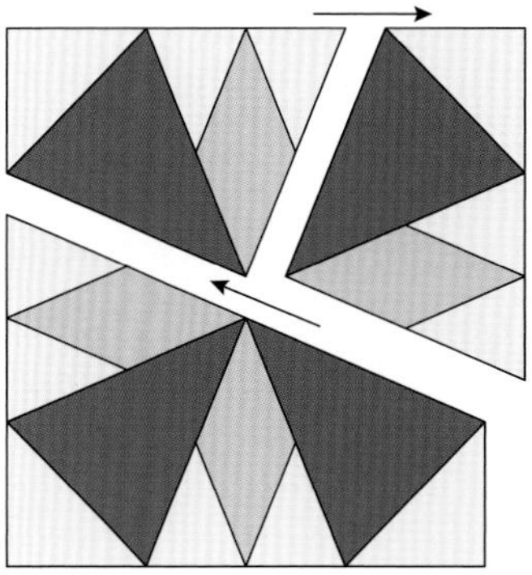

King David's Crown

(Block M-9)

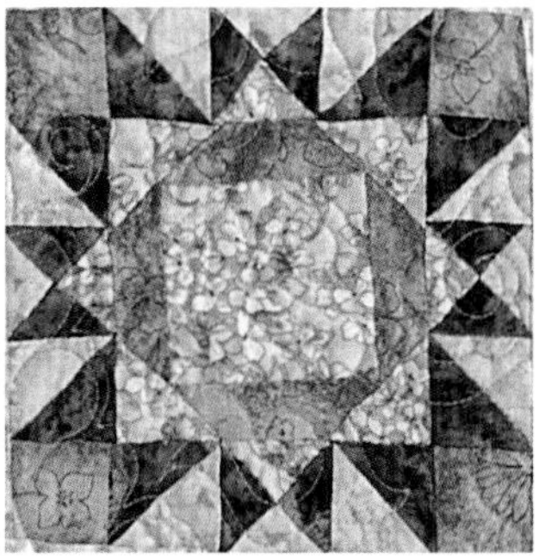

Template patterns are on pages 102 and 103.

1. From background fabric, make 8 triangles using template B and 4 triangles using template C.

2. From medium green fabric, cut 4 triangles using template B, 4 triangles using template C, and 1 square using template D.

3. From blue fabric, make 8 triangles using template B and 8 triangles using template C.

4. From brown fabric, make 4 squares using template A and 4 pieces using template E.

5. Sew the 4 brown E pieces to the green D square. Press. Sew the 4 green B triangles to the corners. Press.

6. Pair each blue B triangle with a background B triangle and sew together along the longest edge to make 8 blue/background triangle-squares. Press.

7. Sew each background C triangle to a blue C triangle along a short edge. Press. Sew each green C triangle to a blue C triangle. Press. Pair each blue/background C unit with a blue/green C unit and sew together to make 4 identical 4-triangle units. Press.

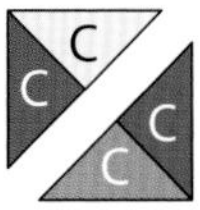

8. Sew 2 triangle-squares from Step 6 to opposite sides of a 4-triangle unit from Step 7. Press. Repeat to make 4.

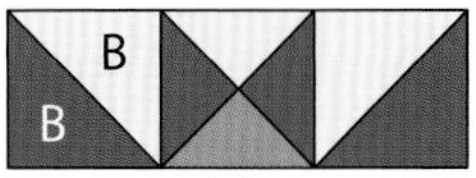

9. Sew 2 units from Step 8 to opposite sides of the central square from Step 5 to make the center row. Press.

10. Sew 2 brown A squares to opposite ends of a unit from Step 8 to make the top row. Press. Repeat to make the bottom row.

11. Sew the 3 rows together. Press.

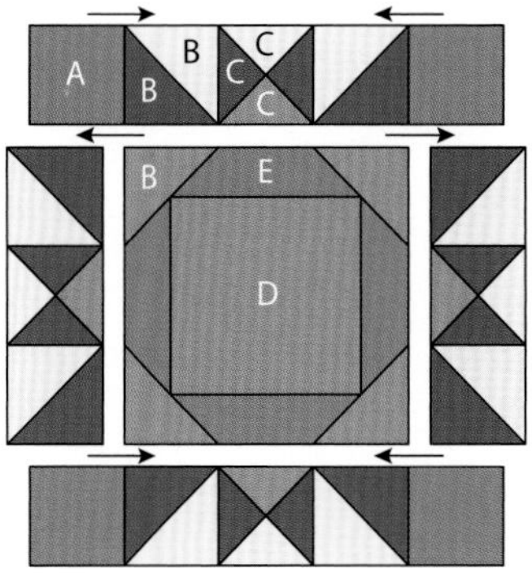

✦ KING'S STAR

Template patterns are on page 104.

1. Make 4 of template A from blue fabric and 4 from brown.

2. Make 4 of template B from blue fabric and 4 from brown.

3. From background fabric, cut 4 squares using template C and 4 triangles using template D.

4. Sew each brown A to a blue B. Sew each blue A to a brown B. Press all toward B. These are the star points.

5. Pair reverse-colored star points from Step 4 and sew together without sewing into the seam allowances. Press. Using Y-seam construction, sew a background square C into the angle created between the star points. Press. Repeat to complete a total of 4 units.

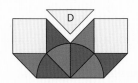

6. Join the star point units from Step 5 in pairs, sewing from point to point only and not into the seam allowances. Press. Using Y-seam construction, sew a background triangle D into the angle created between the star points. Press. Repeat to create 2 star halves.

7. Sew together the 2 star halves from Step 6, sewing from point to point only and not into the seam allowances. Press. Using Y-seam construction, sew a background triangle D into the angles created between the star points. Press.

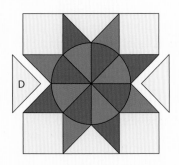

✦ LADIES' AID ALBUM

1. Cut 5 squares 2½″ × 2½″ from brown. Cut 4 rectangles 1½″ × 2½″ from background fabric.

2. Cut 4 squares 1⅞″ × 1⅞″ from dark rose. Cut each square once diagonally to make 8 triangles.

3. Cut 1 square 3¼″ × 3¼″ from light rose. Cut the square twice along the diagonals to make 4 light rose triangles.

4. Pair each light rose triangle with 2 dark rose triangles and sew together to make 4 Flying Geese units. Press.

5. Sew 1 background rectangle to each Flying Geese unit. Press.

6. Sew the Flying Geese units and brown squares into 3 rows as shown. Press. Sew the rows together. Press.

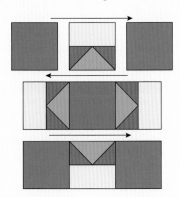

Lady of the Lake

(Block C-5)

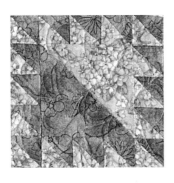

Foundation patterns are on page 104.

1. Make 2 of foundation paper piecing pattern A. Press.

2. Make 1 of foundation paper piecing pattern B. Press. Make 1 of foundation paper piecing pattern B using the reverse of the colors (switch the dark and light blues). Press.

3. Sew the 2 B foundations together. Press. Sew 1 foundation A to the top and 1 foundation A to the bottom as shown. Press.

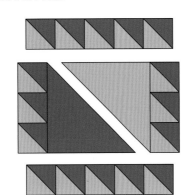

Lancaster Rose

(Block H-6)

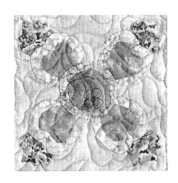

Template patterns are on page 105.

1. Using your favorite appliqué method, prepare 4 leaves from green using template A, 4 outer rose petals from medium red using template B, 4 rose centers from dark red using template C, 1 circle from medium blue using template D, and 1 circle from dark blue using template E. (Note: The templates do *not* include a seam allowance.)

2. Cut 1 square 8″ × 8″ from background fabric.

3. Fold the square in half vertically, horizontally, and diagonally both ways, pressing after each fold to create placement lines.

4. Following the placement diagram on page 105, appliqué the pieces to the background square in alphabetical order: A—leaves, B—outer rose petals, C—rose centers, D—medium blue circle, E—dark blue circle. (If you wish, you can appliqué the A rose centers to the B rose petals and the C circle to the D circle before appliquéing to the background square.) You do not need to appliqué the raw edges covered by other appliqués, but you may want to baste them. Note the overlaps shown in the upper left quadrant of the pattern.

5. Press and trim the square to 6½″ × 6½″.

◈ LAUREL WREATH

(Block I-6)

Template patterns are on pages 104 and 105.

1. From dark green fabric, make 1 square using template D. From background fabric, make 12 triangles using template B. Sew 4 B triangles to the dark green D square. Press after adding each triangle.

2. Cut 8 diamonds from medium green and 8 from brown using template A. Cut 4 squares from background fabric using template C.

3. Sew each green diamond to a brown diamond, sewing only from point to point, not into the seam allowances. Using Y-seam construction, set a B background triangle into the angle. Press. Repeat to make 8 A/B units.

4. Sew together 2 A/B units from Step 3, sewing only from point to point, not into the seam allowances. Using Y-seam construction, set a background C square into the angle. Press. Repeat to create 4 A/B/C units.

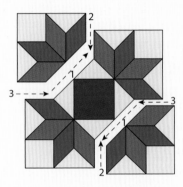

5. Sew 2 A/B/C units to opposite sides of the central square unit created in Step 1, sewing only from point to point and not into the seam allowances. Press.

6. Attach the remaining A/B/C units to the remaining sides of the central square unit, sewing the seams in the order shown.

✦ LEMOYNE STAR

(Block L-7)

Template patterns are on page 106.

1. Using template A, make 4 star points from green fabric and 4 from red. Make 4 triangles from background fabric using template B. Make 4 squares from background fabric using template C.

2. Pair 1 green star point with 1 red star point, right sides together, and sew from point to point, not into the seam allowances. Press. Using Y-seam construction, set a background B triangle into the angle. Press. Make 4.

3. Attach 1 background C square to each green star point, sewing from point to point and not into the seam allowances.

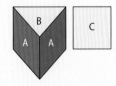

4. Sew together 2 A/A/B/C units, sewing the seams in the direction shown. Stitch from point to point and not into the seam allowances. Press. Repeat to make a second identical unit.

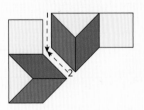

5. Sew the 2 block halves together as shown. Press.

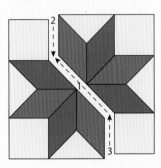

LINCOLN'S PLATFORM

(Block E-8)

Template patterns are on page 107.

1. Cut 4 triangles from background fabric using template A. Cut 4 triangles from blue using template A.

2. Pair each blue triangle with a background triangle, right sides together. Sew along the longest edge to make 4 triangle-squares. Press.

3. Cut 12 squares from green fabric using template B. Cut 8 squares from background fabric using template B.

4. Pair each background square with a green square, right sides together, and sew. Press. Sew the remaining green squares to 4 of the green/background square pairs. Press.

5. Sew a 3-square unit and a 2-square unit to each of the triangle-squares as shown. Press.

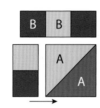

6. Make 4 rectangles from light blue fabric using template C. Join 2 units from Step 5 with a C rectangle to make the top row. Press. Repeat to make the bottom row.

7. Cut 1 square from blue fabric using template B. Sew the remaining 2 C rectangles to opposite sides of the blue square to make the center row. Press.

8. Sew the 3 rows together. Press.

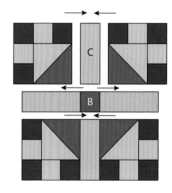

LOG CABIN

(Block H-1)

Foundation pattern is on page 107.

1. Make 1 of the Log Cabin foundation pattern. Press.

✳ LOVE IN A MIST

(*Block G-1*)

1. Cut 1 strip 1⅜″ × 12″ from dark green. Cut 1 strip 1⅜″ × 12″ from light green. Cut 1 strip 1⅜″ × 12″ from dark rose. Cut 1 strip 1⅜″ × 12″ from light rose.

2. Pair the dark green strip with a dark rose strip, right sides together, and sew along the longest edge. Press the seam toward the dark rose fabric. With a rotary cutter, trim off one end of the strip pair at a 45° angle. Cut 4 strips 1⅜″ wide at a 45° angle. (Refer to diagrams on page 20 if needed.)

3. Repeat Step 2 with the light rose strip and the light green strip, but reverse the cutting angle to create mirror images of the pieces created in Step 2. When pressing, press the seams toward the light green fabric.

4. Pair each light strip from Step 3 with a dark strip from Step 2, right sides together. Sew together to make 4 star points, sewing only from point to point and not into the seam allowances. Press.

5. Cut 4 squares 1¾″ × 1¾″ from background fabric. Using Y-seam construction, set the squares into the angles of the star points.

6. Join the star points into 2 pairs. Sew from point to point. Do not sew into the seam allowances. Press.

7. Cut 4 squares 1¾″ × 1¾″ from blue. Cut 2 squares 3″ × 3″ from background fabric. Cut both background squares twice along the diagonal to create 8 background triangles. Sew 2 triangles to each blue square.

8. Set a pieced triangle between the star points of a unit created in Step 6. Repeat to make 2.

9. Sew together the 2 halves of the star. Press. Set the remaining pieced triangles into the angles. Press.

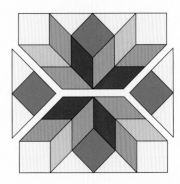

✳ MARINER'S COMPASS

(*Block G-5*)

Template patterns are on page 106.

1. Make 4 of foundation A. Press. Make 4 of foundation B. Press.

2. Pair each foundation A with a foundation B and sew together along the longest side to make a quarter-compass square. Press.

3. Join 2 quarter-compass squares to make a row. Press. Repeat to make a second row. Sew the rows together. Press.

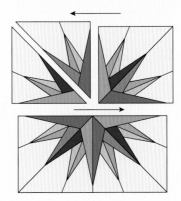

MEXICAN STAR

(Block I-5)

Template patterns are on page 106.

1. From blue fabric, make 4 of template A. From green fabric, make 4 of template B and 4 of template B reverse (Br).

2. Using template C, make 4 squares from background fabric and 1 square from red fabric.

3. From background fabric, make 8 triangles using template D and 4 triangles using template E.

4. Sew 1 D triangle to a green B. Press. Sew 1 E triangle to a B/D unit. Press. Make 4.

5. Sew 1 D triangle to a Br. Press. Sew 1 C square to the Br/D unit. Press. Make 4.

6. Sew together the units from Step 4 and Step 5 to make 4 block side triangles. Press.

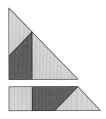

7. Sew 2 block side triangles from Step 6 to opposite sides of a blue A piece to make a row. Press. Repeat to make a second row.

8. Sew 2 blue A pieces to opposite sides of the red C square to make the center row. Press.

9. Sew the 3 rows together. Press.

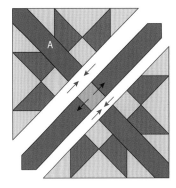

MILKY WAY

(Block D-2)

1. Cut 1 strip 1½″ × 14″ from background fabric and 1 strip 1½″ × 14″ from green. Sew the strips together, right sides facing, along a long side. Press toward the green. Crosscut into rectangles 1½″ wide.

2. Pair the rectangles with right sides together and dark colors facing light. Match the seams and sew along a long side. Press.

3. Cut 2 squares 2⅞″ × 2⅞″ from blue and 2 squares 2⅞″ × 2⅞″ from background fabric. Cut each square once along the diagonal to make 4 blue triangles and 4 background triangles.

4. Pair each background triangle with a blue triangle and sew together along the longest side. Press.

5. Cut 1 square 2½″ × 2½″ from background fabric.

6. Sew the block pieces into 3 rows as shown. Press. Sew the rows together. Press.

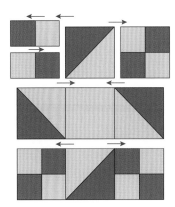

MODERN TULIP

(Block G-9)

Template and foundation patterns are on page 108.

1. Make 4 of foundation pattern A. Press. Make 1 of foundation pattern B. Press.

2. Make 4 parallelograms from light rose using template C. Flip the template and make 4 C reverse (Cr). Repeat with light green fabric to make 4 light green C parallelograms and 4 light green Cr.

3. Pair each light rose C with a light green Cr and sew from point to point, not into the seam allowances. Press. Pair each light rose Cr with a light green C and sew from point to point, not into the seam allowances. Press. (Be sure to follow the diagram for correct color placement.)

4. Cut 2 squares 2¼″ × 2¼″ from background fabric. Cut each square twice diagonally to make 8 background triangles. Using Y-seam construction, set the background triangles into the angles between the light rose and light green parallelograms.

5. Pair the mirror-image parallelogram units, right sides together, and sew from point to point along the light rose edge. Do not sew into the seam allowances. Press.

6. Using Y-seam construction, set the A foundations into the angles between the mirror-image parallelogram units. Press.

7. Cut 2 squares 1⅞″ × 1⅞″ from dark green. Cut each square once diagonally to make 4 dark green triangles. Sew 1 dark green triangle to each unit from Step 6. Press.

8. From background fabric, cut 4 squares 2½″ × 2½″.

9. Sew the squares and units into 3 rows as shown. Press. Sew the rows together. Press.

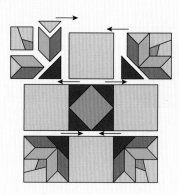

MOSAIC NO. 3

(Block A-1)

Foundation patterns are on page 110.

1. Make 1 each of foundation patterns A, B, and C. Press.

2. Sew foundation A to foundation B. Press.

3. Sew foundation C to foundation A/B. Press.

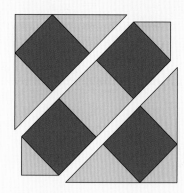

✴ MOTHER'S DELIGHT

(Block D-3)

Foundation patterns are on page 109.

1. Make 4 each of foundation patterns A and B. Press.

2. Pair each foundation A with a foundation B and sew together. Press.

3. Arrange the foundations as shown and sew into 2 rows. Press.

4. Sew the rows together. Press.

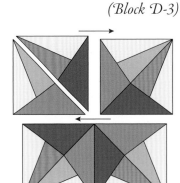

◈ MOTHER'S FAVORITE

(Block L-2)

Foundation patterns are on page 108.

1. Make 1 of foundation pattern A. Press. Make 4 of foundation pattern B. Press.

2. Attach 2 B foundations to opposite sides of the A foundation. Press.

3. Sew the remaining B foundations to the remaining opposite sides of the A foundation. Press.

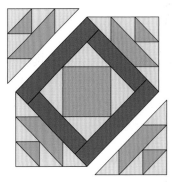

▨ MRS. CLEVELAND'S CHOICE

(Block B-8)

Template and foundation patterns are on page 109.

1. Make 1 of foundation pattern A. Press. Make 4 each of foundation patterns B, E, and F. Press.

2. Sew the 4 B foundations to the A foundation. Press after each addition.

3. Make 2 rectangles C and 2 rectangles D from blue fabric. Sew to the A/B square. Press.

4. Pair each E foundation with an F foundation and sew together to make 4 corner triangles. Press. Attach to the A/B/C/D square. Press.

New Mexico

(Block M-7)

Template and foundation patterns are on pages 108 and 109.

1. Make 1 of foundation pattern A, using the colorway brown-background-brown. Press. Crosscut into 8 strips $^{15}/_{16}''$ wide.

2. Make 2 of foundation pattern A, using the colorway background-brown-background. Using template C as a guide, cut 1 strip set into 4 pieced squares. From the remaining strip set, crosscut 4 strips $^{15}/_{16}''$ wide.

3. Sew 2 strips from Step 1 to a strip from Step 2 to make a nine-patch. Repeat to make 4.

4. Using template B, make 12 triangles from background fabric, 8 triangles from blue, and 4 triangles from brown. Pair each blue and each brown triangle with a background triangle and sew together along the longest side to make 8 blue/background triangle-squares and 4 brown/background triangle-squares. Press.

5. Using template C, make 4 squares from blue and 1 square from brown.

6. Arrange the block units into 5 rows as shown. Press. Sew the rows together. Press.

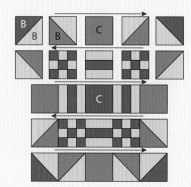

 # Night & Noon

(Block C-10)

1. Make 2 of foundation pattern A. Press. Make 1 each of foundation patterns B and C. Press.

2. Sew foundation B to foundation C. Press. Attach the A foundations to opposite sides of the B/C unit as shown. Press.

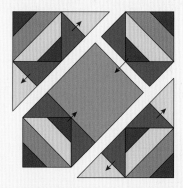

New York Beauty

(Block F-5)

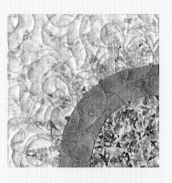

Template and foundation patterns are on pages 112 and 113.

1. Make 1 wedge from light green using template A. Make 1 arc from green using template B. Make 1 corner from background fabric using template C. Be sure to mark the center points to make it easier to align the pieces.

2. Make 1 pieced arc foundation using brown and background fabrics. Press.

3. Sew arc B to wedge A. Press. Sew corner C to the pieced arc. Press. Sew the 2 sections together. Press.

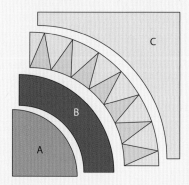

NINE-PATCH

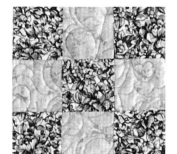

1. Cut 5 squares 2½″ × 2½″ from red fabric.

2. Cut 4 squares 2½″ × 2½″ from background fabric.

3. Arrange the blocks in checkerboard fashion. Sew into 3 rows. Press.

4. Sew the 3 rows together, matching seams. Press.

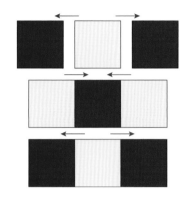

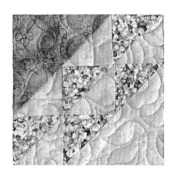 NORTHWIND

Foundation patterns are on page 114.

1. Make 1 each of foundation patterns A and B. Press.

2. Sew the 2 foundations together. Press.

OCEAN WAVES

1. Cut 6 squares 2¾″ × 2¾″ from background fabric. Cut each square in half diagonally twice to make 24 background triangles (light triangles).

2. Cut 6 squares 2¾″ × 2¾″ from assorted blue and green fabrics. Cut each square in half diagonally twice to make 24 blue and green triangles (dark triangles).

3. Pair 12 light triangles with 12 dark triangles and sew together along the longest edge to make 12 triangle-squares. Press.

4. Sew 2 triangle-squares together. Press. Sew 1 light triangle and 1 dark triangle to opposite ends. Press. Make 2.

5. Repeat Step 4 to make 2 additional units, placing lights and darks as shown.

6. Sew a dark triangle to a triangle-square. Press. Add a second dark triangle. Press. Make 2.

7. Sew a light triangle to a remaining triangle-square. Press. Repeat. Add a second light triangle. Press. Make 2.

8. Sew each remaining light triangle to a dark triangle along a short side to make 2 block corner tips and 2 mirror-image block corner tips. Press. Sew each corner tip to one of the strips from Steps 4 and 5 to make 4 corner triangles, following the diagram for color placement. Press.

9. Cut 1 square 3½″ × 3½″ from medium blue fabric. Attach the 2 triangles from Step 6 to opposite sides of the square, following the diagram for color placement. Press. Attach the 2 triangles from Step 7 to the remaining sides of the square. Press.

10. Sew the corner triangles to opposite sides of the central unit as shown. Press.

1. From background fabric, cut:

- 8 A squares 1¼″ × 1¼″.

- 8 squares 1⅝″ × 1⅝″.
  Cut each in half diagonally once
  to make 16 small background B
  triangles.

- 2 squares 2¾″ × 2¾″.
  Cut each in half diagonally twice
  to make 8 large background C
  triangles.

- 1 D square 2″ × 2″.

2. From blue fabric, cut 12 squares
1⅝″ × 1⅝″. Cut each in half diagonally
once to make 24 small blue B triangles.

3. From red fabric, cut:

- 4 A squares 1¼″ × 1¼″.

- 1 square 2¾″ × 2¾″.
  Cut in half diagonally twice to
  make 4 large red C triangles.

4. From green fabric, cut 4 squares
2⅜″ × 2⅜″. Cut each square in half
diagonally once to make 8 green E
triangles.

5. Pair 8 blue B triangles with 8 small
background B triangles to make 8
triangle-squares. Press. Sew 4 triangle-
squares to background A squares and 4
to red A squares. Press. Pair the background square units with red square
units and sew together to make 4 corner
units. Press.

6. Sew 2 blue B triangles to each large
background C triangle to make 8
Flying Geese units. Press.

7. Sew 2 Flying Geese units to opposite
sides of the large background D square.
Press. Sew 2 background A squares each
to opposite ends of 2 additional Flying
Geese. Press. Sew these 3 rows together
to make the central star. Press.

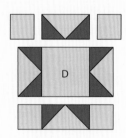

8. Sew 2 background B triangles each
to opposite ends of the remaining
Flying Geese units. Press. Sew a red C
triangle to each unit. Press. Sew 2 green
E triangles to each unit. Press.

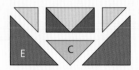

9. Sew 2 units from Step 8 to opposite
sides of the central star. Press.

10. Sew 2 corner units to opposite sides
of the remaining 2 units created in Step
8 to make the top and bottom rows.
Press. Sew the 3 rows together. Press.

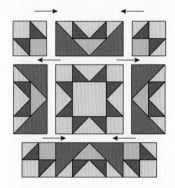

◈ ODD FELLOW'S PATCH

(Block D-6)

1. Make 2 of foundation pattern A, 1 of B, and 1 of C. Press.

2. Sew foundation B to foundation C. Press.

3. Sew the A foundations to opposite sides of the B/C unit. Press.

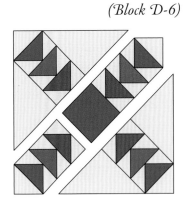

Foundation patterns are on page 113.

◈ OHIO STAR

(Block M-5)

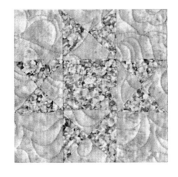

1. Cut 1 square 2½″ × 2½″ from blue fabric for the center of the block.

2. Cut 4 squares 2½″ × 2½″ from background fabric for the block corners.

3. Cut 2 squares 3¼″ × 3¼″ from background fabric. Cut 2 squares 3¼″ × 3¼″ from blue fabric. Make 4 quick-pieced triangle-squares (see page 22, Step 2) from the squares. Press.

4. Make 4 quick-pieced quarter-square triangle units from the half-square triangles created in Step 3.

a. On the wrong side of a half-square triangle unit, draw a diagonal line from a dark corner to a light corner.

b. Place another half-square triangle unit together with the unit with the drawn line, right sides facing and dark triangles facing light triangles. Align edges, abut opposing seams, and pin.

c. Sew with a ¼″ seam allowance on both sides of the drawn line. Cut on the drawn line to make 2 quarter-square triangle units. Press.

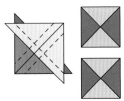

d. Repeat Steps a–c to make 2 more quarter-square triangle units.

5. Arrange and sew the segments into 3 rows as shown. Press. Sew the rows together. Press.

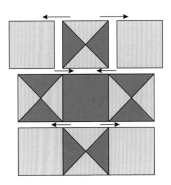

OKLAHOMA DOGWOOD

(Block G-2)

Template and foundation patterns are on page 115.

1. Cut 1 strip 2″ × 12″ from dark blue and 1 strip 2″ × 12″ from background fabric. Place the strips together, right sides facing, and sew along the longest edge. Press.

2. Crosscut 4 strips 2″ wide from the blue/background strip. Pair 2 of these strips, opposite colors together, and sew along the longest side to make a four-patch. Press. Repeat with the remaining strips to make a second four-patch.

3. Make 2 of the foundation-pieced unit. Press.

4. Make 2 wedges from background fabric using template A. Make 2 arcs from background fabric using template B. Sew a wedge and an arc to each foundation-pieced arc, matching the centers. Press.

5. Sew the units into 2 rows as shown. Press. Sew the rows together. Press.

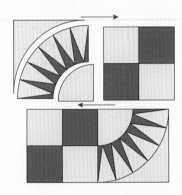

OLD MAID'S PUZZLE

(Block F-4)

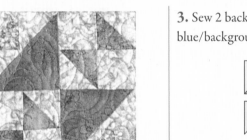

1. Cut 5 squares 2⅜″ × 2⅜″ from background fabric. Cut 2 squares 2⅜″ × 2⅜″ from brown. Cut 1 square 2⅜″ × 2⅜″ from blue. Cut each square once along the diagonal to make 10 background triangles, 4 brown triangles, and 2 blue triangles.

2. Pair each blue triangle and each brown triangle with a background triangle and sew together along the longest side to make 2 blue/background triangle-squares and 4 brown/background triangle-squares. Press.

3. Sew 2 background triangles to each blue/background triangle-square. Press.

4. Cut 1 square 3⅞″ × 3⅞″ from green. Cut once along the diagonal to make 2 triangles. Sew 1 green triangle to each unit from Step 3. Press.

5. Cut 4 squares 2″ × 2″ from background fabric. Sew 1 square to a brown edge of each brown/background triangle-square. Press.

6. Pair 2 units from Step 5, matching seams. Sew along a long side. Press. Make 2.

7. Sew the units into 2 rows as shown. Press. Sew the rows together. Press.

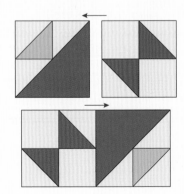

ORANGE PEEL

Option 1: Template Piecing

Template patterns are on page 115.

1. Make 4 of template A from background fabric. Make 4 of template B from brown fabric.

2. Sew 2 B's to 1 A. Press. Repeat to make a second B/A/B unit.

3. Sew 2 A's to a B/A/B unit. Press.

4. Sew the remaining B/A/B unit to the unit from Step 3. Press.

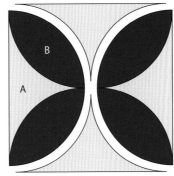

Option 2: Appliqué

Template pattern is on page 115.

1. Cut an 8″ × 8″ square from background fabric. Fold the square in half vertically and horizontally and along both diagonals to find the center; mark placement lines.

2. Using your favorite appliqué method, prepare 4 "peels" from red fabric using template B. (Note: The template includes a seam allowance.)

3. Using the diagram and the fold lines in the square to determine placement, appliqué the 4 B pieces to the background square.

4. Press and trim the block to 6½″ × 6½″.

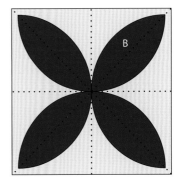

PINEAPPLE

Foundation pattern is on page 116.

1. Make 1 of the Pineapple foundation pattern. Press.

PINWHEEL 1

1. From background fabric, cut 2 squares 3⅞″ x 3⅞″. From brown fabric, cut 2 squares 3⅞″ x 3⅞″.

2. Make 4 quick-pieced brown/background triangle-squares (see page 22, Step 2). Press.

3. Sew the triangle-squares into 2 rows as shown. Press. Sew the rows together. Press.

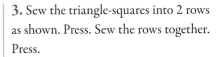

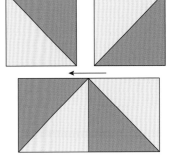

✦ PINWHEEL 2

(Block J-7)

Template pattern is on page 116.

1. From background fabric, make 4 trapezoids using template A.

2. From background fabric, cut 1 square 4¼″ × 4¼″. Cut the square in half diagonally twice to make 4 background triangles. Repeat with blue fabric and green fabric.

3. Pair each blue triangle with a background triangle and sew together along a short side. Press.

4. Pair each green triangle with a background trapezoid A and sew together along a short side. Press.

5. Join each blue triangle unit from Step 3 to a green triangle unit from Step 4 to create a block quarter. Press.

6. Sew the block quarters into 2 rows. Press. Sew the rows together. Press.

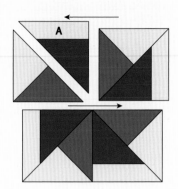

✦ POSIES 'ROUND THE SQUARE

(Block A-4)

Template patterns are on page 117.

1. From blue fabric, cut 4 quarter circles using template B. From background fabric, cut 1 using template A and 4 using template C.

2. Sew 4 B quarter circles to the central shape A. Press.

3. Using your favorite appliqué method, appliqué the flowers to the C triangles. Press. Make 4. (Note: The flower appliqué shapes do *not* include a seam allowance.)

4. Sew the triangles to the unit from Step 2. Press.

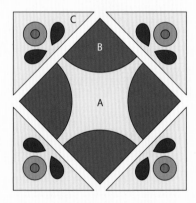

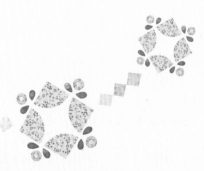

PROVIDENCE

Template patterns are on page 117.

1. From blue fabric, cut 4 squares using template A and 8 triangles using template B.

2. From background fabric, cut 1 square 2¼″ × 2¼″. Cut in half twice diagonally to make 4 small E triangles.

3. From dark green fabric, make 1 of template A and 8 of template B.

4. Make 4 of template C from medium green fabric.

5. Make 4 of template D from red fabric.

6. Sew the 4 small background E triangles to the dark green A square. Press.

7. Sew 2 blue B triangles to opposite sides of each red D piece. Press.

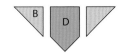

8. Sew 1 dark green triangle to each blue A square. Press. Sew 1 dark green triangle to each medium green C piece. Press. Sew each B/A unit to a B/C unit. Press.

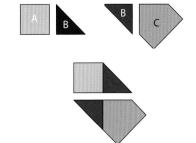

9. Sew 2 of the units from Step 8 to opposite sides of the unit from Step 6 to make the center row. Press.

10. Sew 2 units from Step 7 to opposite sides of each remaining unit from Step 8 to make the top and bottom rows. Press.

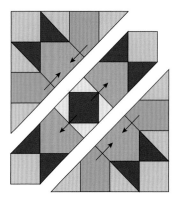

11. Sew the diagonal rows together. Press.

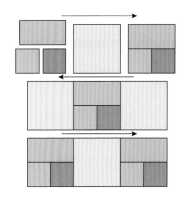

PUSS IN THE CORNER

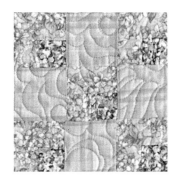

1. From background fabric, cut 4 squares 2½″ × 2½″.

2. From blue fabric, cut 5 rectangles 2½″ × 1½″ and 1 strip 14″ × 1½″.

3. From brown fabric, cut 1 strip 14″ × 1½″. Pair with the blue strip, right sides together, and sew along a long edge. Press. Crosscut into 5 strips 1½″ wide.

4. Sew each blue/brown strip to a blue rectangle. Press.

5. Sew the block units into 3 rows. Press. Sew the rows together. Press.

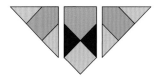

(Block E-9)

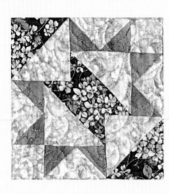

Template patterns are on page 118.

1. Make 8 triangles from green using template A. Make 4 triangles from background fabric using template B. Sew 2 green A triangles to each background B triangle to make 4 Flying Geese units. Press.

2. Make 2 squares from background fabric using template C. Sew 1 C square to the right side of a Flying Geese unit. Press. Make 2.

3. Make 2 triangles from red using template D. Make 4 triangles from background fabric using template D. Pair each dark triangle with a light triangle and sew together along the longest side to make 2 triangle-squares. Press.

4. Make 2 trapezoids from red using template E. Sew each remaining D triangle to a red trapezoid. Press.

5. Sew 1 Flying Geese unit to each D/E unit. Press. Sew 1 Flying Geese/C unit to each Flying Geese/D/E unit. Press.

6. Sew the 2 triangle-squares from Step 3 to a unit from Step 5. Attach the remaining unit, sewing the seams in the order shown. Sew point to point only, do not sew into the seam allowances.

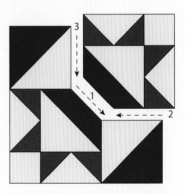

(Block D-4)

1. Make 2 of foundation pattern A. Press. Make 1 each of foundation patterns B and C. Press.

2. Sew foundation B to foundation C. Press.

3. Sew the A foundations to opposite sides of the B/C unit. Press.

Foundation patterns are on page 119.

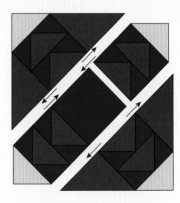

RIBBON STAR

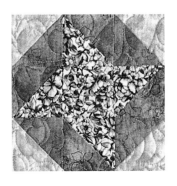

1. Cut 2 squares 2⅞″ × 2⅞″ from light green. Cut 2 squares 2⅞″ × 2⅞″ from blue. Cut each square once along the diagonal to make 4 light green triangles and 4 blue triangles.

2. Pair each light green triangle with a blue triangle and sew together along the longest side. Press.

3. Cut 2 squares 2⅞″ × 2⅞″ from green. Cut 2 squares 2⅞″ × 2⅞″ from background fabric. Cut each square once along the diagonal to make 4 green triangles and 4 background triangles.

4. Pair each green triangle with a background triangle and sew together along the longest side. Press.

5. Cut 1 square 2½″ × 2½″ from light green.

6. Sew the block segments into 3 rows. Press. Sew the rows together. Press.

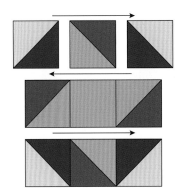

RIGHT HAND OF FRIENDSHIP

1. From red fabric, cut 1 square 2⅞″ × 2⅞″. Cut in half once diagonally to make 2 large red triangles. Repeat with blue fabric to make 2 large blue triangles.

2. Pair each large red triangle with a large blue triangle and sew together along one of the short edges. Sew the 2 pieced triangles together to make the central square. Press.

3. From red fabric, cut 1 square 3¼″ × 3¼″. Cut in half twice diagonally to make 4 small red triangles. Repeat with blue fabric to make 4 small blue triangles. Repeat with background fabric to make 4 small background triangles.

4. Sew each small red triangle to a small background triangle along a short edge. Press.

5. From background fabric, cut 4 squares 2½″ × 2½″.

6. Sew 2 small blue triangles to adjacent sides of 2 background squares. Press. Sew these units to opposite sides of the central square. Press.

7. Sew 2 red/background triangles to adjacent sides of the 2 remaining background squares. Press. Attach these units to opposite sides of the central square unit. Press.

ROAD TO OKLAHOMA

1. From background fabric, cut 4 squares 2″ × 2″. Repeat with green fabric and brown fabric.

2. From background fabric, cut 2 squares 2⅜″ × 2⅜″. Cut each square in half diagonally once to make 4 background triangles. Repeat with green fabric to make 4 green triangles.

3. Pair each green triangle with a background triangle and sew together along the longest edge to make 4 triangle-squares. Press.

4. Sew the squares and triangle-squares into 4 rows. Press. Sew the rows together. Press.

(Block K-1)

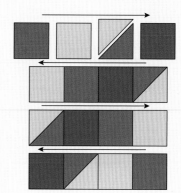

ROBBING PETER TO PAY PAUL

Template patterns are on page 118.

1. Using template A, make 2 from green fabric and 2 from background fabric.

2. Using template B, make 8 from green fabric and 8 from background fabric.

3. Matching the center lines, sew 4 background B's to 1 green A. Press. Repeat to make 2.

4. Matching the center lines, sew 4 green B's to 1 background A. Press. Repeat to make 2.

5. Sew the 4 units into 2 rows. Press. Sew the rows together. Press.

(Block D-7)

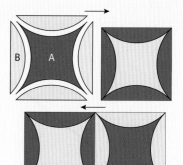

ROCKY ROAD TO DUBLIN

Template patterns are on page 118.

1. Using template A, make 8 arcs from background fabric and 8 arcs from red.

2. Using template B, make 8 quarter circles from green and 8 quarter circles from background fabric.

3. Matching lights with darks, pair each A arc with a B quarter circle and sew together. Press.

4. Sew the units into 4 rows. Press. Sew the rows together. Press.

(Block I-10)

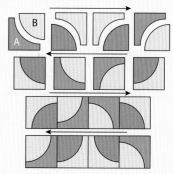

ROLLING STAR

Template patterns are on page 119.

1. Using template A, make 4 star points from green, 4 star points from light red, and 8 star points from brown.

2. From background fabric, make 8 squares using template B.

3. From light brown fabric, make 4 triangles using template C.

4. Sew 1 background square to each green and light red diamond, sewing from point to point only and not into the seam allowances. Press.

5. Sew 1 light red A/B unit to 1 dark green A/B unit, stitching from point to point only and not into the seam allowances. Sew the seams in the direction shown. Press. Repeat to make 4 star quarters.

6. Join the star quarters into pairs to make 2 star halves, stitching from point to point only and not into the seam allowances. Sew the seams in the direction shown. Press.

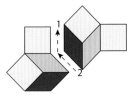

7. Join the block halves to complete the central star, stitching from point to point only and not into the seam allow-

ances. Sew the seams in the direction and order shown. Press.

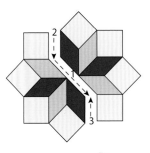

8. Using Y-seam construction, attach the brown A pieces to the background squares. Press.

9. Sew the light brown C triangles to the 4 corners. Press.

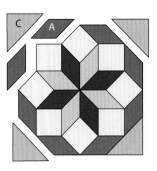

ROLLING STONE

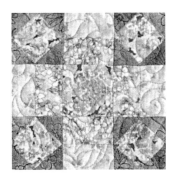

Template pattern is on page 119.

1. From background fabric, cut 4 B rectangles 1½″ × 2½″. Repeat with light green fabric. Pair each light green B rect-

angle with a background B rectangle and sew together along a long edge. Press.

2. From light brown fabric, cut 1 C square 2½″ × 2½″. Sew 2 B/B rectangle pairs to opposite sides of the C square to make the center row.

3. From light brown fabric, cut 4 squares using template A.

4. From blue fabric, cut 6 squares 1⅞″ × 1⅞″. Cut each square in half diagonally once to make 12 blue D triangles. Repeat with 2 green squares 1⅞″ × 1⅞″ to make 4 green D triangles.

5. Sew 3 blue D triangles and 1 green D triangle to each small light brown A square. Press.

6. Sew the block units into 3 rows. Press. Sew the rows together. Press.

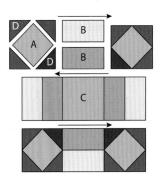

❖ Rosebud

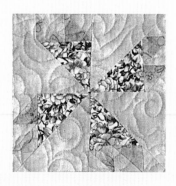

Option 1:
Traditional Piecing

1. Cut 6 squares 1⅞″ × 1⅞″ from background fabric. Cut each square once diagonally to make 12 A triangles.

2. Cut 4 squares 1⅞″ × 1⅞″ from red fabric. Cut each square once diagonally to make 8 A triangles.

3. Pair each red triangle with a background triangle and sew together along the longest edge. Press.

4. Pair 2 red/background triangle-squares, right sides together, and sew. Press. Attach 1 more background

triangle. Press. Repeat to make 4 rows of 5 triangles.

5. Cut 2 squares 2⅞″ × 2⅞″ from green fabric. Cut each square once diagonally to make 4 green B triangles.

6. Attach 1 green B triangle to each unit from Step 4. Press.

7. Cut 2 squares 3⅞″ × 3⅞″ from background fabric. Cut each square once diagonally to make 4 C triangles.

8. Sew 1 background C triangle to each unit created in Step 6.

9. Sew the units created in Step 8 into 2 rows. Press. Sew the rows together. Press.

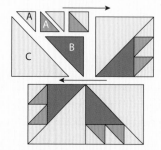

Option 2:
Foundation Paper Piecing

Foundation pattern is on page 120.

1. Make 4 of the foundation pattern. Press.

2. Sew the foundations into 2 rows. Press. Sew the rows together. Press.

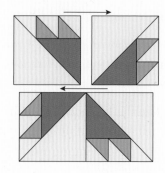

❖ Sarah's Choice

1. Cut 4 A squares 2″ × 2″ from background fabric.

2. Cut 1 square 4¼″ × 4¼″ from background fabric. Cut in half twice diagonally to make 4 B background triangles.

3. Cut 4 squares 2⅜″ × 2⅜″ from dark blue fabric. Cut each square in half once diagonally to make 8 dark blue C triangles. Repeat with light blue fabric to make 8 light blue C triangles.

4. Pair 4 dark blue C triangles with 4 light blue C triangles and sew together along the longest edge to make 4 triangle-squares. Sew the triangle-squares into 2 rows and sew the rows together, pinwheel fashion, to make the center of the block.

5. Sew 1 light blue C triangle and 1 dark blue C triangle to each background B triangle to make 4 Flying Geese units.

6. Sew the units and A squares into 3 rows. Press. Sew the 3 rows together. Press.

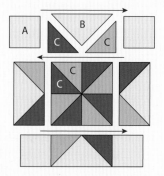

SARAH'S FAVORITE

Template pattern is on page 120.

1. Using template A, make 10 squares from dark green fabric and 10 squares from medium green fabric.

2. From dark green, cut 1 square 2¾″ × 2¾″. Cut diagonally twice to make 4 B triangles. Repeat using medium green fabric.

3. Cut 1 square 4¼″ × 4¼ from background fabric. Cut diagonally twice to make 4 C triangles.

4. Sew 2 dark green A squares and 2 medium green A squares together to make a four-patch. Press. Repeat to make a total of 5 four-patch units.

5. Sew 3 four-patch units together to make a row. Press.

6. Sew 2 background C triangles to opposite sides of a four-patch block. Press. Repeat to make 2.

7. Sew the 3 rows together. Press.

8. Pair each medium green triangle with 1 dark green triangle and sew together to make 4 medium/dark green triangle units. Press. (Make 2 with the medium green triangle on the left and the dark green on the right; then make 2 mirror-image units.)

9. Attach the medium/dark green triangle units to the corners. Press.

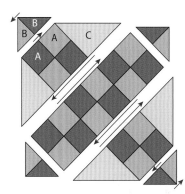

SAWTOOTH STAR

Template pattern is on page 120.

1. Cut 4 B squares 2″ × 2″ from background fabric.

2. Cut 1 square 4¼″ × 4¼″ from background fabric. Cut in half twice diagonally to make 4 background C triangles.

3. Cut 1 A square 2⅝″ × 2⅝″ from green fabric.

4. Cut 4 squares 2⅜″ × 2⅜″ from green fabric. Cut each square in half once diagonally to make 8 green D triangles. Repeat with 2 squares of light red fabric to make 4 light red D triangles.

5. Sew the 4 light red D triangles to the green A square. Press.

6. Sew 2 green D triangles to each background triangle to make 4 Flying Geese units. Press.

7. Sew the units into 3 rows. Press. Sew the 3 rows together. Press.

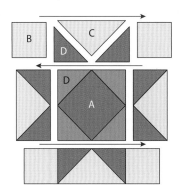

◆ SHOO-FLY

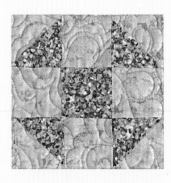

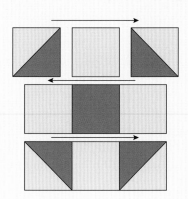

1. From brown fabric, cut 2 squares 2⅞″ × 2⅞″. From background fabric, cut 2 squares 2⅞″ × 2⅞″.

2. Make 4 quick-pieced brown/background triangle squares (see page 22, Step 2).

3. From background fabric, cut 4 squares 2½″ × 2½″. From brown fabric, cut 1 square 2½″ × 2½″.

4. Sew the block segments into 3 rows as shown. Press. Sew the rows together. Press.

◆ SICKLE

1. Cut 1 strip 1¼″ × 12″ from light green fabric and 1 strip 1¼″ × 12″ from light red. Pair the strips, right sides together, and sew along a long edge. Press. Crosscut into 8 strips 1¼″ wide.

2. Join the strips together in pairs, opposite colors facing, and sew along the longest edges to make 4 four-patches.

3. From brown fabric, cut 4 squares 2″ × 2″. Sew 1 brown square to each four-patch from Step 2. Press.

4. Join the units from Step 3 into pairs and sew along a long edge to make 2 double four-patches.

5. From dark green fabric, cut 1 square 3⅞″ × 3⅞″. Cut once diagonally to make 2 dark green triangles. Repeat with background fabric.

6. Pair each dark green triangle with a background triangle and sew together along the longest edge to make 2 triangle-squares. Press.

7. Sew the block segments into 2 rows. Press. Sew the rows together. Press.

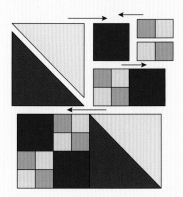

SILVER AND GOLD

Template patterns are on page 120.

1. Cut 1 strip 2″ × 40″ from brown and 1 from green. With right sides together, sew the strips along the long edge. Press the seam open.

2. Make 8 diamonds from freezer paper using template A. Iron the freezer-paper templates to the wrong side of the brown/green strip pair, aligning the central line with the seam. Cut out 8 two-color star points.

3. Join the star points into 4 pairs. Sew from point to point. Do not sew into the seam allowances. Press.

4. From background fabric, cut 4 squares using template B. Using Y-seam construction, set the B squares between the star points, sewing from point to point and not into the seam allowances. Press.

5. Sew together 2 units from Step 4. Set a C triangle between the star points. Press. Repeat to make 2.

6. Sew together the 2 units from Step 5. Using Y-seam construction, set the remaining C triangles into the angles. Press.

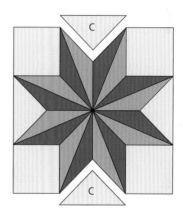

SISTER'S CHOICE

Template patterns are on page 121.

1. Make 8 triangles from background fabric using template A. Make 8 triangles from blue fabric using template

A. Pair each blue triangle with a background triangle, right sides together, and sew along the longest edge. Press.

2. Make 4 squares from background fabric using template B. Make 5 squares from blue fabric using template B.

3. Make 4 rectangles from green fabric using template C.

4. Join 1 blue B square, 1 background B square, and 2 blue/background triangle-squares to make a star point. Press. Repeat to make 4 total.

5. Join the units from Step 4, the green C rectangles, and the remaining blue B square into 3 rows. Press. Sew the 3 rows together. Press.

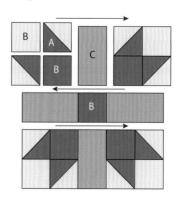

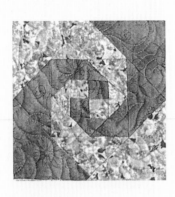

Template pattern is on page 120.

1. From background fabric, cut:

- 2 squares 1¼″ × 1¼″.

- 2 triangles using template A.

- 1 square 2³/₈″ × 2³/₈″.
  Cut in half once diagonally to
  make 2 B triangles.

- 1 square 3″ × 3″.
  Cut in half once diagonally to
  make 2 C triangles.

- 1 square 3⁷/₈″ × 3⁷/₈″. Cut in half
  once diagonally to make 2 D
  triangles.

2. Repeat Step 1 using green fabric.

3. Pair each background square with
a green square and sew together. Press.
Sew the pairs together to make the
center four-patch. Press.

4. Following the diagram for color
placement, sew the background A triangles to opposite sides of the four-patch.
Press. Sew the green A triangles to the
remaining sides. Press.

5. Following the diagram for color
placement, sew the background B triangles to opposite sides of the central
unit. Press. Sew the green B triangles to
the remaining sides. Press.

6. Following the diagram for color
placement, sew the background C triangles to opposite sides of the central
unit. Press. Sew the green C triangles to
the remaining sides. Press.

7. Following the diagram for color
placement, sew the background D triangles to opposite sides of the central
unit. Press. Sew the green D triangles to
the remaining sides. Press.

Spinning Hourglass

Template patterns are on page 121.

1. From background fabric, make 4 of template A and cut 1 square 2¾″ × 2¾″. Cut the square in half twice diagonally to make 4 background C triangles.

2. From green fabric, cut 1 square 2¾″ × 2¾″. Cut in half twice diagonally to make 4 green C triangles. Cut 2 squares 3⅛″ × 3⅛″. Cut each in half once diagonally to make 4 large green D triangles.

3. From dark blue fabric, make 1 square using template B. Cut 2 squares 2¾″ × 2¾″. Cut in half twice diagonally to make 8 dark blue C triangles.

4. From medium blue, cut 2 squares 3⅛″ × 3⅛″. Cut each in half once diagonally to make 4 medium blue D triangles.

5. Pair each small background C triangle with a dark blue C triangle and sew together along the longest edge to make 4 triangle-squares. Press. Attach a small green C triangle to each triangle-square. Press.

6. Sew each remaining dark blue C triangle to a background A piece. Press. Attach a medium blue D triangle to each. Press.

7. Sew each unit created in Step 5 to a unit created in Step 6. Press.

8. Following the diagram, sew the units created in Step 7 to the dark blue B square in numerical order, using the partial seams piecing method:

a. When attaching the first unit, sew only part of the way along the edge, as indicated by the arrow.

b. Sew units 2 through 4, using a complete seam. You will need to fold the first unit out of the way in order to sew on the fourth unit.

c. After attaching the fourth unit, complete the partial seam for the first unit.

9. Sew a large medium green D triangle to each corner. Press.

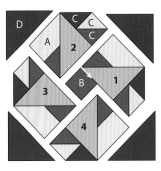

Square and Star

Foundation patterns are on page 121.

1. Make 4 of foundation paper piecing pattern A. Press. Make 2 of foundation paper piecing pattern B. Press. Make 1 of foundation paper piecing pattern C. Press.

2. Sew the 2 B foundations to the central C foundation. Press.

3. Sew 2 A foundation corners to opposite sides of the B/C/B unit. Press. Sew on the remaining A foundations. Press.

STAMP BASKETS

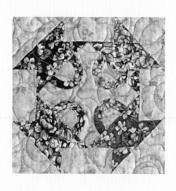

Template pattern is on page 122.

1. Cut 4 background squares 2⅞″ × 2⅞″. Cut each square once along the diagonal to make 8 background A triangles.

2. From each of 4 basket print fabrics, cut 1 square 2⅞″ × 2⅞″. Cut each square once along the diagonal to make 8 basket print A triangles, 2 of each color. (You will use only 1 triangle of each basket print. Set the other triangle aside for another project.)

3. Cut 1 square 1⅞″ × 1⅞″ from each of the 4 basket prints. Cut each square once along the diagonal to make 8 small C triangles, 2 of each color.

4. Cut 8 background D squares 1½″ × 1½″.

5. Using your favorite appliqué method, make 1 handle from each of the 4 basket prints using template B. (Note: Template B does *not* include any seam allowances.)

6. Using the template as a placement diagram, appliqué the basket handles to 4 of the background triangles from Step 1. The seam allowances along the bottom straight edges of the handles will fall into the seam allowance of the background triangle and do not need to be appliquéd down. Press.

7. Matching the prints, pair the basket print A triangles from Step 2 with the triangles from Step 6. Sew together along the long edge. Press.

8. Sew the small print C triangles to the small background D squares, creating mirror-image units as shown for each basket. Press.

9. Matching the prints, sew the units from Step 8 to the units from Step 7. Press.

10. Sew a background A triangle to each basket. Press. Sew the baskets into 2 rows. Press. Sew the rows together. Press.

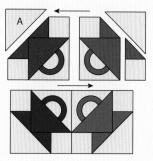

STAR OF THE ORIENT

Template and foundation patterns are on page 122.

1. Make 4 each of the star point foundation patterns A and B. Press.

2. Make 1 central octagon using template C. Press.

3. Sew the star points to the central octagon in numerical order as shown, using the partial seams piecing method:

- When attaching the first point which is a foundation A, sew only part of the way along the edge, as indicated by the arrow.

- Sew on star points 2 through 8, alternating A and B foundations, using a complete seam. You will need to fold the first star point out

of the way in order to sew on the eighth star point.

- After attaching the eighth star point, complete the partial seam for the first star point.

4. Press after adding each star point.

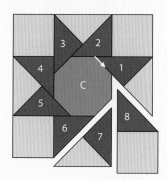

STEPS TO THE ALTAR

(Block L-6)

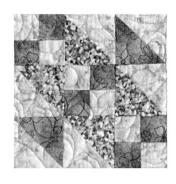

1. Cut 1 strip 1½″ × 12″ from background fabric and 1 strip 1½″ × 12″ from blue. Place the strips right sides together and sew along a long edge. Press toward the blue fabric.

2. Crosscut 6 strips 1½″ wide from the strip set. Join the strips together in pairs, right sides and opposite colors facing, and sew together along a long edge to make 3 four-patches. Press.

3. From blue fabric, cut 1 square 2⅞″ × 2⅞″. From brown fabric, cut 2 squares 2⅞″ × 2⅞″. From background fabric, cut 3 squares 2⅞″ × 2⅞″.

4. Make 2 quick-pieced triangle-square units (see page 22, Step 2) from the 2⅞″ × 2⅞″ background and blue squares. Make 4 quick-pieced triangle-square units from the background and brown squares. Press.

5. Arrange the block segments into 3 rows. Press. Sew the rows together. Press.

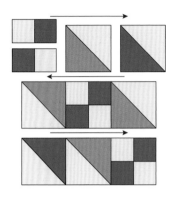

SWAMP PATCH

(Block B-7)

1. Cut 1 square 2½″ × 2½″ from dark green fabric for the center of the block.

2. Cut 2 squares 2⅞″ × 2⅞″ from light green fabric and 2 squares 2⅞″ × 2⅞″ from background fabric. Cut each square once on the diagonal to make 4 light green triangles and 4 background triangles.

3. Pair each light green triangle with a background triangle. Sew along the longest edge to make 4 triangle-squares. Press.

4. From background fabric, cut 2 squares 3¼″ × 3¼″. From dark green fabric, cut 2 squares 3¼″ × 3¼″.

5. Make 4 quick-pieced triangle-square units (see page 22, Step 2) from the background and dark green squares from Step 4. Press toward the darker fabric.

6. Make 4 quick-pieced quarter-square triangle units from the triangle-squares from Step 5:

   a. On the wrong side of a triangle-square, draw a diagonal line from a dark corner to a light corner.

   b. Pair another triangle-square with the one with the drawn line, right sides facing and dark triangles facing light triangles. Align edges, abut opposing seams, and pin.

   c. Sew with a ¼″ seam allowance on both sides of the drawn line. Cut on the drawn line to make

2 quarter-square triangle units. Press.

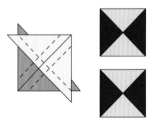

   d. Repeat Steps a–c for the other 2 half-square triangle units.

7. Sew the segments into 3 rows. Press. Sew the 3 rows together. Press.

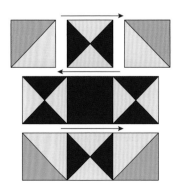

(Block H-5)

Foundation pattern is on page 122.

1. From blue fabric, cut 2 rectangles 2¾″ × 3½″ and 3 squares 1¼″ × 1¼″.

2. Cut 4 squares 1⅝″ × 1⅝″ from background fabric. Cut each square in half once diagonally to make 8 background triangles. Repeat with tan fabric to make 8 tan triangles.

3. Pair a background triangle with a tan triangle and sew along the longest side to make a triangle-square. Press. Repeat to make a total of 4 triangle-squares.

4. Sew the triangle-squares from Step 3 together to make a pinwheel unit. Press.

5. Cut 2 squares 2¾″ × 2¾″ from blue fabric. Cut the square in half twice diagonally to make 4 blue triangles. Sew 1 tan triangle and 1 background triangle to each blue triangle to make 4 Flying Geese. Refer to the block diagram for color placement. Press.

6. Sew 2 Flying Geese to opposite sides of the pinwheel unit. Press. Sew 2 blue squares to opposite ends of 1 Flying Geese unit. Press. Sew this unit to the top of the pinwheel unit. Press. Sew 1

blue rectangle to the left side of the pinwheel unit. Press.

7. Sew the remaining blue square to the remaining Flying Geese unit. Press. Attach the remaining blue rectangle as shown. Press.

8. Complete foundation A. Press.

9. Sew the units into 2 rows. Press. Sew the rows together. Press.

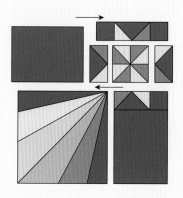

(Block A-6)

Foundation pattern is on pages 122 and 123.

1. Make 8 star points using the foundation pattern.

2. Join the star points into 4 pairs. Sew from point to point only. Do not sew into the seam allowance. Press.

3. From background fabric, cut 4 squares using template A and 4 triangles using template B.

4. Using Y-seam construction, set A squares between the star point pairs, sewing from point to point and not into the seam allowance. Press.

5. Join 2 of the units from Step 4. Using Y-seam construction, set a B triangle between the star points. Press. Repeat to make 2.

6. Sew the 2 units from Step 5 together. Using Y-seam construction, set the remaining B triangles into the angles. Press.

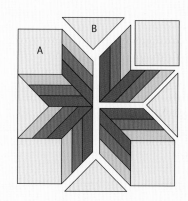

THE FRIENDSHIP QUILT

(Block K-2)

Foundation pattern is on page 123.

1. From background fabric, cut 4 squares 2⅜″ × 2⅜″. Cut each square in half diagonally once to make 8 background A triangles.

2. From dark blue fabric, cut 4 B squares 2″ × 2″. Sew 2 background triangles to each square to make 4 large corner triangles. Press.

3. Complete the foundation pattern. Press.

4. Sew 2 corner triangles to opposite sides of the foundation. Press. Attach the remaining 2 corner triangles to the remaining sides. Press.

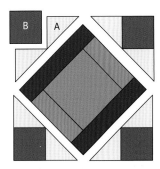

TRIP AROUND THE WORLD

(Block J-2)

Option 1: Foundation Paper Piecing

Foundation pattern is on page 123.

1. Make and press 5 rows using the foundation pattern and the following color placement:

- Dark blue, light green, medium blue, light green, dark blue: Make 2.

- Light green, medium blue, light red, medium blue, light green: Make 2.

- Medium blue, light red, brown, light red, medium blue: Make 1.

2. Sew the rows together. Press.

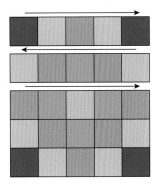

Option 2: Template Piecing

Template pattern is on page 123.

Using template A, cut 4 dark blue squares, 8 light green squares, 8 medium blue squares, 4 light red squares, and 1 brown square. Sew the squares into rows. Press. Sew the rows together. Press.

TRUE LOVER'S KNOT

(Block I-1)

Template patterns are on page 123.

1. Make 4 squares from dark blue using template A.

2. Using template B, make 8 partial squares from medium green and 8 from background fabric.

3. Sew 2 medium green B's to opposite sides of each A square. Sew from point to point only and not into the seam allowances. Press toward A. Repeat to make 4.

4. Using Y-seam construction, attach the background fabric B's to opposite sides of the A squares and to adjacent sides of the dark green B's. Sew the seams in the order and direction shown. Press toward the darker fabrics. Repeat to make 4.

5. Sew the units into 2 rows. Press. Sew the rows together. Press.

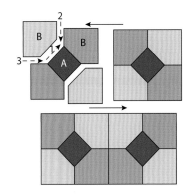

Template pattern is on page 124.

1. Using template A, make 7 diamonds from light brown fabric, 7 diamonds from medium green fabric, and 7 diamonds from dark blue fabric.

2. Sew each medium green diamond to a dark blue diamond, sewing only from point to point and not into the seam allowances. Press.

3. Using Y-seam construction, set a light brown diamond between each green and blue diamond. Make 7. Press.

4. Choose a "block" for the center. Sew 3 other blocks to the center block, sewing only from point to point and not into the seam allowances. Press.

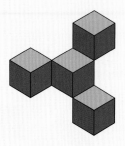

5. Using Y-seam construction, sew the remaining blocks to the center unit. Sew the seams in the order and direction shown. Press.

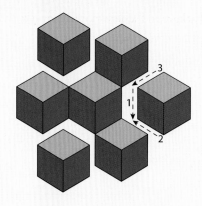

6. Cut 1 square 8″ × 8″ from background fabric. Fold and press vertically, horizontally, and twice diagonally to mark the center of the square.

7. Fold under the seam allowances of the 7-block unit, center the unit on the background square, and appliqué in place. Carefully trim away the extra fabric behind the appliqué, if desired.

8. Press and trim the block to 6½″ × 6½″.

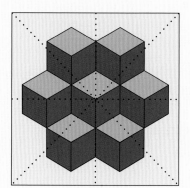

WEATHERVANE

Template pattern is on page 124.

1. From red fabric, cut 4 of template A.

2. From background fabric, cut:

- 4 D squares 1½″ × 1½″.

- 8 squares 1⅞″ × 1⅞″.
  Cut each square in half diagonally once to make 16 B triangles.

3. From blue fabric, cut:

- 1 F square 2½″ × 2½″.

- 4 E squares 1½″ × 1½″.

- 4 squares 1⅞″ × 1⅞″.
  Cut each square in half diagonally once to make 8 C triangles.

4. Pair each blue C triangle with a background B triangle. Sew together along the longest edge to make 8 triangle-squares. Press.

5. Sew 1 triangle-square to each small background D square. Press toward the square. Sew 1 triangle-square to each small blue E square. Press toward the square. Pair each blue square unit with a background square unit as shown to make 4 corner units. Press.

6. Sew 2 small background B triangles to each red A. Press.

7. Sew the units into 3 rows. Press. Sew the rows together. Press.

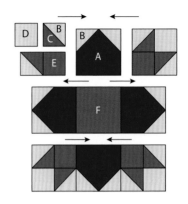

WEDDING RING 1

Foundation patterns are on page 124.

1. Make 2 of foundation pattern A. Press.

2. Make 2 of foundation pattern B. Press.

3. Make 1 of foundation pattern C. Press.

4. Sew the rows together. Press.

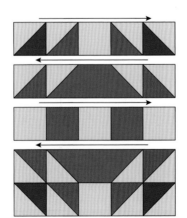

WEDDING RING 2

(Block H-2)

Template pattern is on page 124.

1. Cut 2 squares 2⅞" × 2⅞" from background fabric. Cut each square in half once diagonally to make 4 large background B triangles.

2. Cut 2 squares 2⅛" × 2⅛" from background fabric. Cut each square in half once diagonally to make 4 small background C triangles.

3. Make 4 of template A from red fabric. Sew a large background B triangle to the longest side and a small background C

triangle to the second-longest side. Press toward A. Make 4 corner units.

4. Cut 4 D rectangles 1½" × 1¾" from red fabric.

5. Cut 2 E rectangles 1½" × 1¾" from blue fabric. Sew a red D rectangle to each. Press. Repeat to make 2.

6. Cut 1 F rectangle 1½" × 4" from blue. Sew a red D rectangle to each end. Press.

7. Sew the units into 3 rows. Press. Sew the rows together. Press.

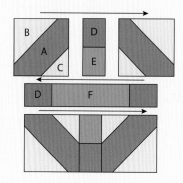

WILD GOOSE CHASE

(Block M-2)

Foundation patterns are on page 125.

1. Make 2 of foundation paper piecing pattern A. Press. Make 1 of foundation paper piecing pattern B. Press. Make 1 of foundation paper piecing pattern C. Press.

2. Sew the B foundation to the C foundation. Press.

3. Sew the A foundations to opposite sides of the B/C unit. Press.

WINDBLOWN SQUARE

(Block N-5)

1. From background fabric, cut 8 squares 2⅜" × 2⅜".

2. From brown fabric, cut 4 squares 2⅜" × 2⅜". From blue fabric, cut 4 squares 2⅜" × 2⅜".

3. Make 8 quick-pieced triangle-square units (see page 22, Step 2) from 4 each of the blue and background fabric squares. Make 8 more quick-pieced triangle-square units from the remaining 4 background squares and the 4 brown squares. Press.

4. Join the blue triangle-squares together in pairs as shown. Press. Join the brown triangle-squares together in pairs as shown. Press.

5. Sew each blue triangle-square pair to a brown triangle-square pair to make a block quarter as shown. Press.

6. Sew the block quarters into 2 rows. Press. Sew the rows together. Press.

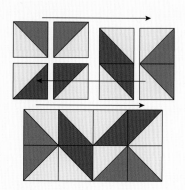

❖ WINDING WAYS

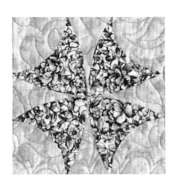

Template patterns are on pages 124 and 125.

1. Make 4 of template A from red fabric. From background fabric, make 4 of template B and 4 of template C.

2. Sew each red A to a background B, matching the centers. Press toward A.

3. Sew 2 A/B units to opposite sides of a background C. Press toward A. Repeat to create a second row.

4. Sew 2 background C's to one of the rows. Press toward A.

5. Sew the remaining row to the unit from Step 4. Press.

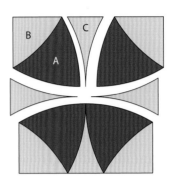

❖ YANKEE PUZZLE

1. Cut 2 squares 4¼″ × 4¼″ from background fabric. Cut 2 squares 4¼″ × 4¼″ from red.

2. From the background and red squares, make 4 quick-pieced triangle-square units (see page 22, Step 2). Press.

3. Make 4 quick-pieced quarter-square triangle units from the triangle-square from Step 2:

　a. On the wrong side of a triangle-square, draw a diagonal line from a dark corner to a light corner.

　b. Pair another triangle-square with the one with the drawn line, right sides facing and dark triangles facing light triangles. Align edges, abut opposing seams, and pin.

　c. Sew with a ¼″ seam allowance on both sides of the drawn line. Cut on the drawn line to make 2 quarter-square triangle units. Press.

　d. Repeat Steps a–c to make 2 more quarter-square triangle units.

4. Arrange the quarter-square triangle units into 2 rows as shown. Press. Sew the rows together. Press.

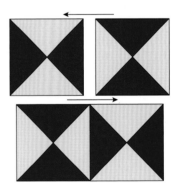

General Instructions

SASHING AND BORDERS

Cutting

Beige: Cut 5 strips 6½″ wide. Cut into 130 short sashing strips 1½″ × 6½″.

Cut 23 strips 1½″ wide. Sew diagonally end to end. Cut 9 long sashing strips 1½″ × 97½″.

Cut 6 strips 1½″ wide. Sew diagonally end to end. Cut 2 strips 1½″ × 97½″ for the inner long borders.

Cut 4 strips 1½″ wide. Sew the strips together in pairs with diagonal seams. Cut a 1½″ × 71½″ strip from each pair for the inner short borders.

Dark green: Cut 6 strips 2½″ wide. Sew diagonally end to end. Cut 2 strips 2½″ × 99½″ for the middle long borders.

Cut 4 strips 2½″ wide. Sew the strips together in pairs with diagonal seams. Cut a 2½″ × 75½″ strip from each pair for the middle short borders.

Medium blue: Cut 6 strips 6½″ wide. Sew diagonally end to end. Cut 2 strips 6½″ × 103½″ for the outer long borders.

Cut 6 strips 6½″ wide. Sew diagonally end to end. Cut 2 strips 6½″ × 87½″ for the outer short borders.

QUILT ASSEMBLY

1. Arrange the sampler blocks in 10 rows of 14 blocks. Sew the blocks together with short sashing strips. Press the seams toward the sashing strips. (**Note:** If any of the blocks have an obvious up-and-down orientation, decide whether you prefer a vertical or horizontal orientation for your quilt and arrange all directional blocks accordingly.)

2. Sew the sampler block rows together, separated by the long sashing strips. Press toward the sashing strips.

3. Sew the long beige inner borders to the long sides of the quilt. Press toward the border. Sew the short beige inner borders to the short sides of the quilt. Press toward the border.

4. Sew the long dark green middle borders to the long sides of the quilt. Press toward the green border. Sew the short dark green middle borders to the short sides of the quilt. Press toward the green border.

5. Sew the long medium blue outer borders to the long sides of the quilt. Press toward the blue border. Sew the short medium blue outer borders to the short sides of the quilt. Press toward the blue border.

6. Refer to your favorite basic quilting book to layer the quilt top, batting, and backing. Baste. Quilt as desired. Attach a hanging sleeve, and bind. (**Note:** If you are using signature squares, these can be pieced together to make the quilt backing.)

7. If you did not use signature squares for the quilt backing, make a panel that includes the names of all the block contributors. Appliqué this panel to the back of the quilt.

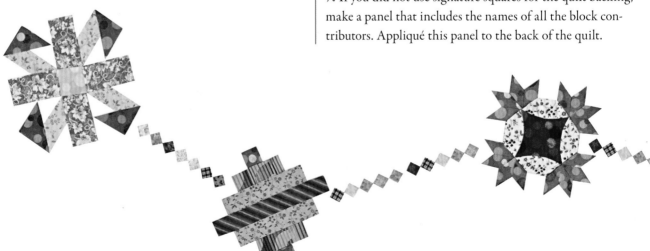

A1	A2	A3	A4	A5	A6	A7	A8	A9	A10
B1	B2	B3	B4	B5	B6	B7	B8	B9	B10
C1	C2	C3	C4	C5	C6	C7	C8	C9	C10
D1	D2	D3	D4	D5	D6	D7	D8	D9	D10
E1	E2	E3	E4	E5	E6	E7	E8	E9	E10
F1	F2	F3	F4	F5	F6	F7	F8	F9	F10
G1	G2	G3	G4	G5	G6	G7	G8	G9	G10
H1	H2	H3	H4	H5	H6	H7	H8	H9	H10
I1	I2	I3	I4	I5	I6	I7	I8	I9	I10
J1	J2	J3	J4	J5	J6	J7	J8	J9	J10
K1	K2	K3	K4	K5	K6	K7	K8	K9	K10
L1	L2	L3	L4	L5	L6	L7	L8	L9	L10
M1	M2	M3	M4	M5	M6	M7	M8	M9	M10
N1	N2	N3	N4	N5	N6	N7	N8	N9	N10

Quilt Assembly Diagram

The Gallery

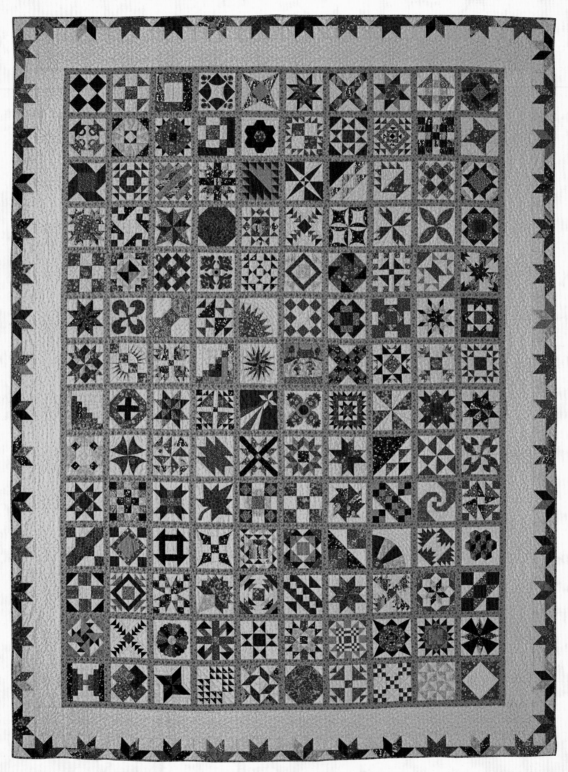

SYLVIA'S BRIDAL SAMPLER, 89″ × 115″,
hand pieced and hand quilted by Annelies van den Bergh,
2008, The Netherlands

CHAIN OF FRIENDS, *89½″ × 104½″,*
pieced and appliquéd by Trisha Chubbs, quilted by Lou Sawyer,
2008, USA

CHAINING UP THE BLUES, 96″ × 96″,
pieced and appliquéd by Caroline Van Maele-Delbrouck,
quilted by Valérie Langue, 2008, Belgium

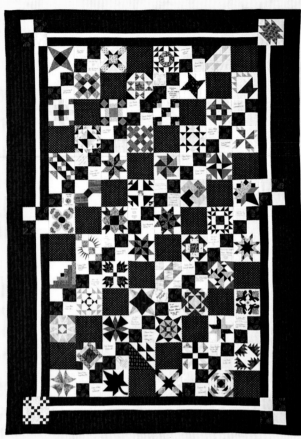

STITCHING THE BLUES AWAY WITH MY FRIENDS,
68″ × 93″, pieced and appliquéd by Elise Fare and friends, quilted
by Elise Fare, 2008, USA

SYLVIA'S BRIDAL SAMPLER, 98″ × 118″,
pieced and appliquéd by Tanya Anderson, 2008, USA

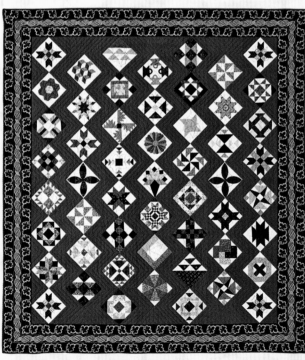

A LITTLE GUY IN A BLUE WORLD, 68½″ × 76″,
pieced, appliquéd, and quilted by Valérie Langue, 2008, USA

SYLVIA'S BRIDAL SAMPLER—
MY JOURNEY WITH SYLVIA, 88" × 111",
pieced, appliquéd, and quilted by Anne Ida Røkeness,
2008, Norway

Template and Foundation

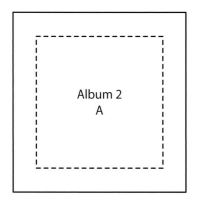

Album 2
A

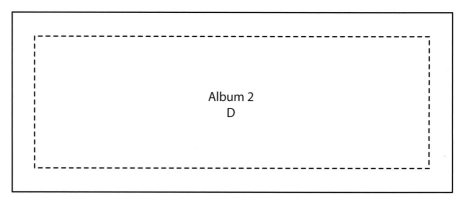

Album 2
D

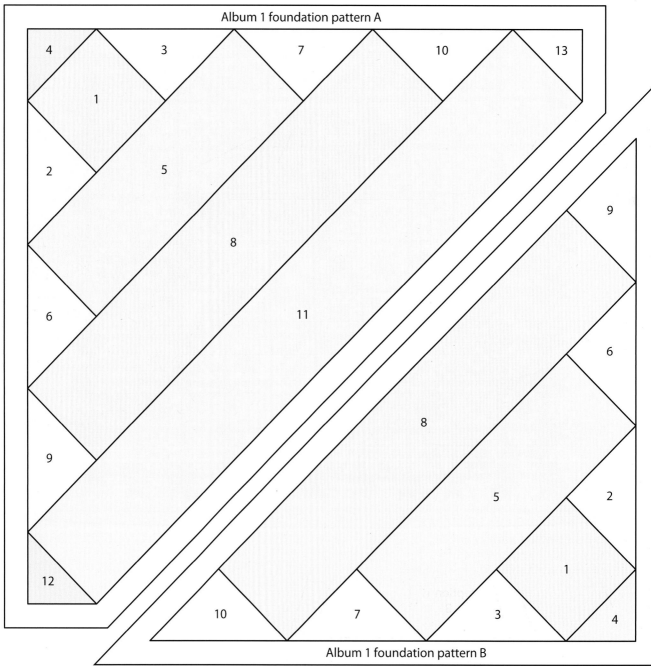

Album 1 foundation pattern A

Album 1 foundation pattern B

Patterns

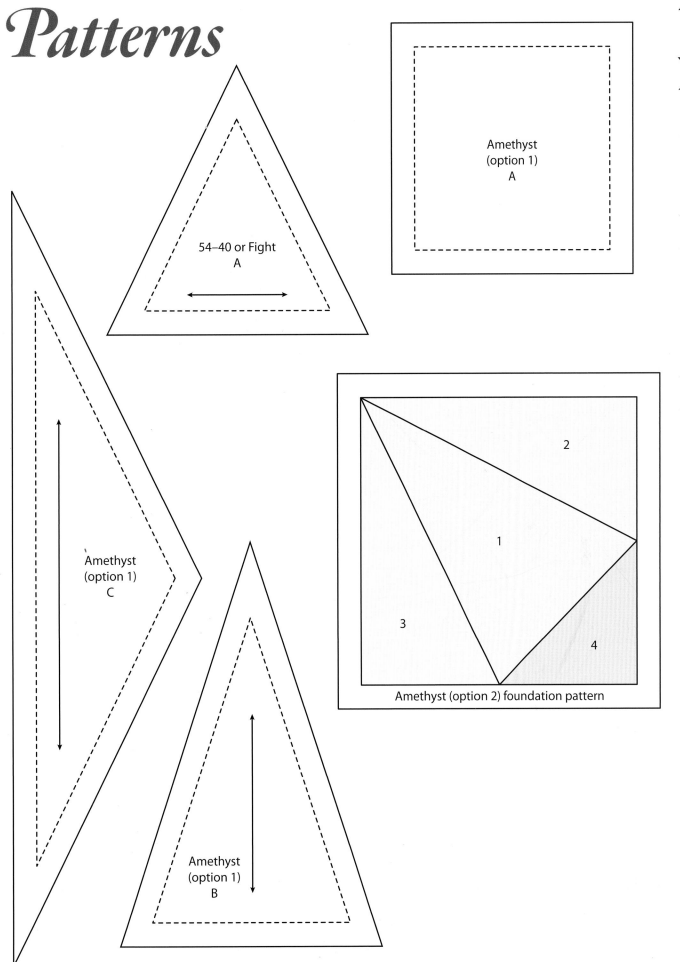

54–40 or Fight
A

Amethyst
(option 1)
A

Amethyst
(option 1)
C

Amethyst
(option 1)
B

1

2

3

4

Amethyst (option 2) foundation pattern

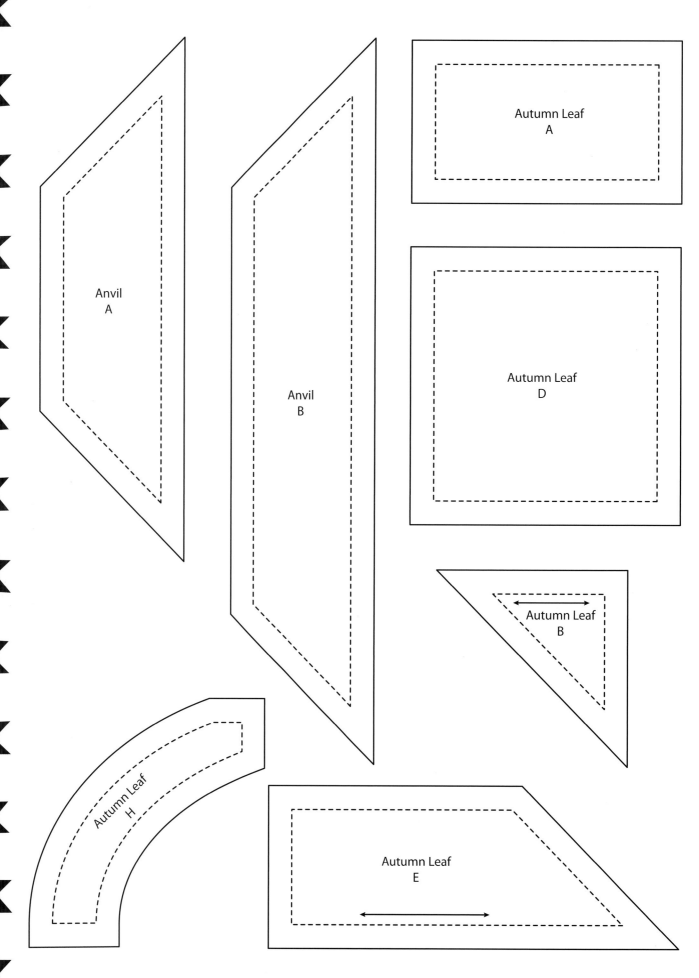

Anvil
A

Anvil
B

Autumn Leaf
A

Autumn Leaf
D

Autumn Leaf
B

Autumn Leaf
H

Autumn Leaf
E

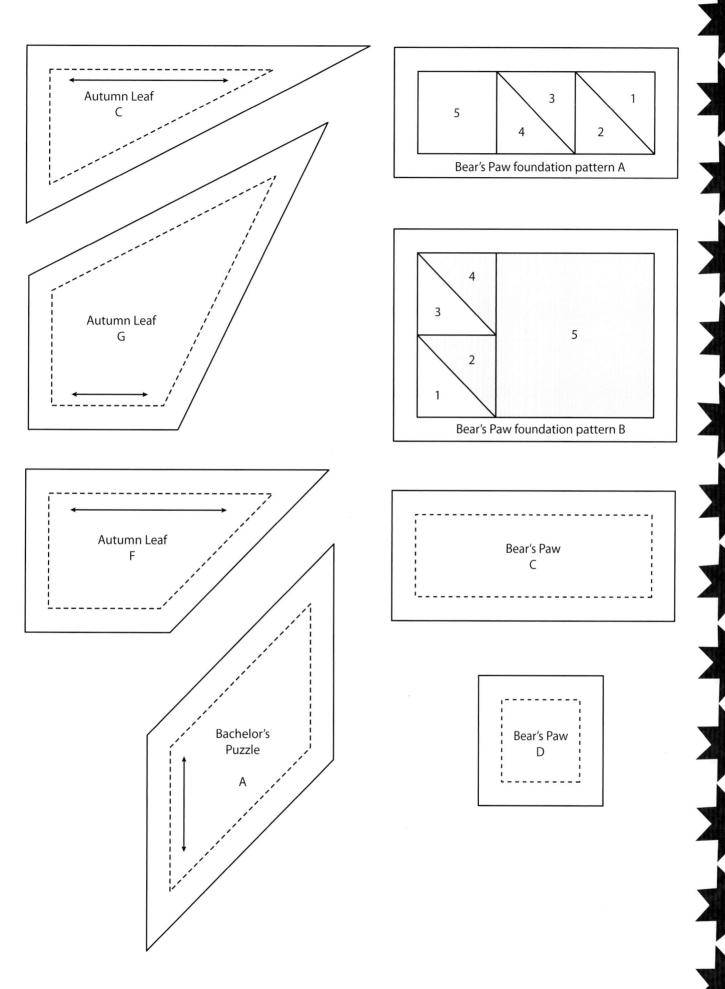

Autumn Leaf
C

Autumn Leaf
G

Autumn Leaf
F

Bachelor's
Puzzle

A

Bear's Paw foundation pattern A

5

3

1

4

2

Bear's Paw foundation pattern B

4

3

2

1

5

Bear's Paw
C

Bear's Paw
D

TEMPLATE AND FOUNDATION PATTERNS   87

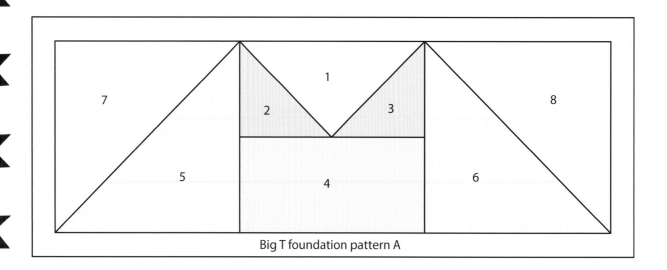

Big T foundation pattern A

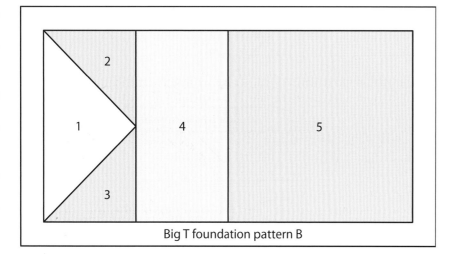

Big T foundation pattern B

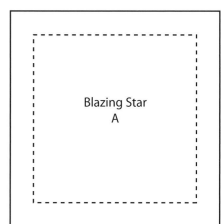

Blazing Star
A

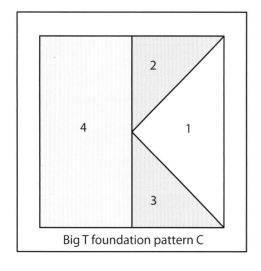

Big T foundation pattern C

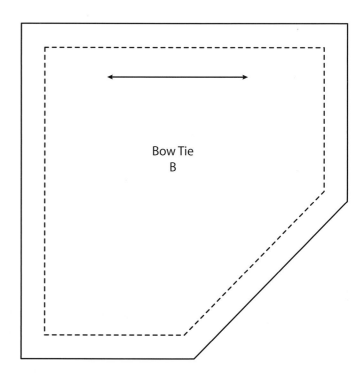

Bow Tie
B

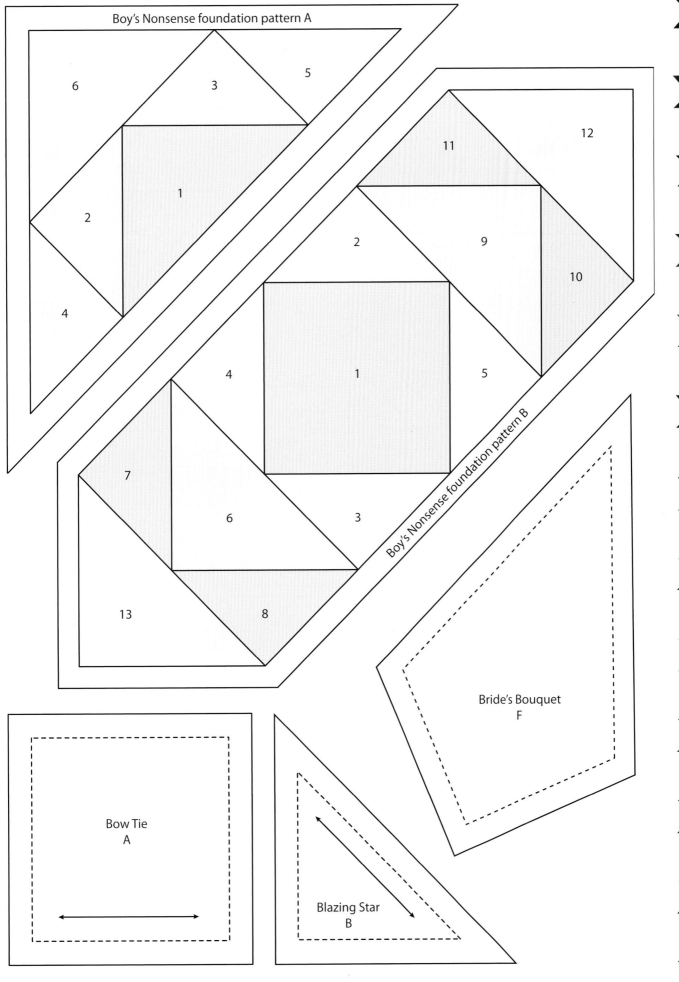

Boy's Nonsense foundation pattern A

6 3 5

1

2

4

Boy's Nonsense foundation pattern B

11 12

2 9

10

4 1 5

7

6 3

13 8

Bride's Bouquet
F

Bow Tie
A

Blazing Star
B

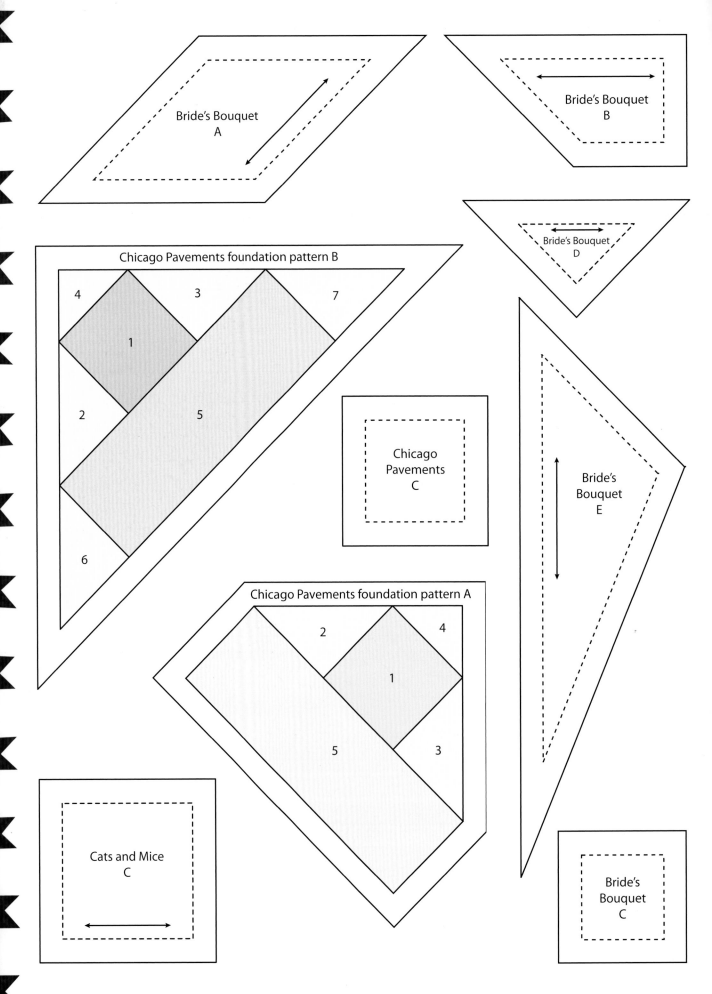

Bride's Bouquet
A

Bride's Bouquet
B

Bride's Bouquet
D

Chicago Pavements foundation pattern B

4 3 7
1
2 5
6

Chicago
Pavements
C

Bride's
Bouquet
E

Chicago Pavements foundation pattern A

2 4
1
5 3

Cats and Mice
C

Bride's
Bouquet
C

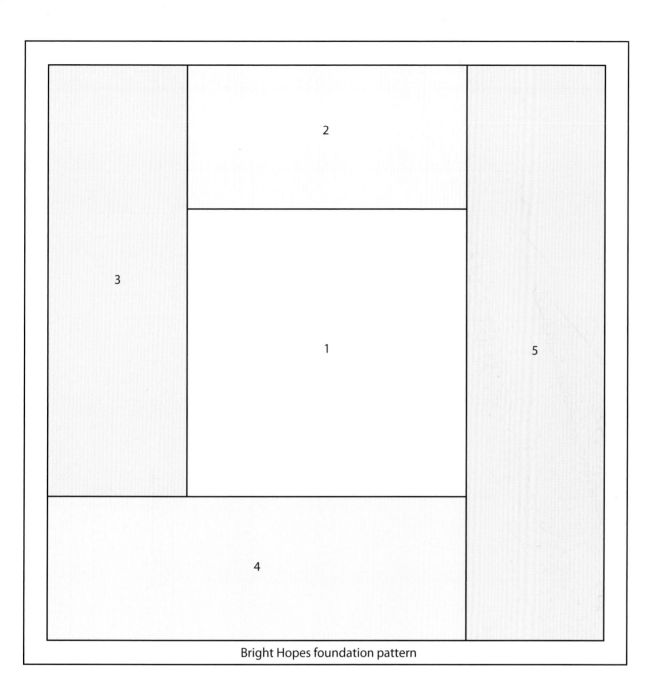

Bright Hopes foundation pattern

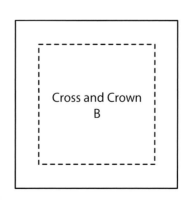

Cross and Crown foundation pattern

Cross and Crown
B

Cross and Crown
A

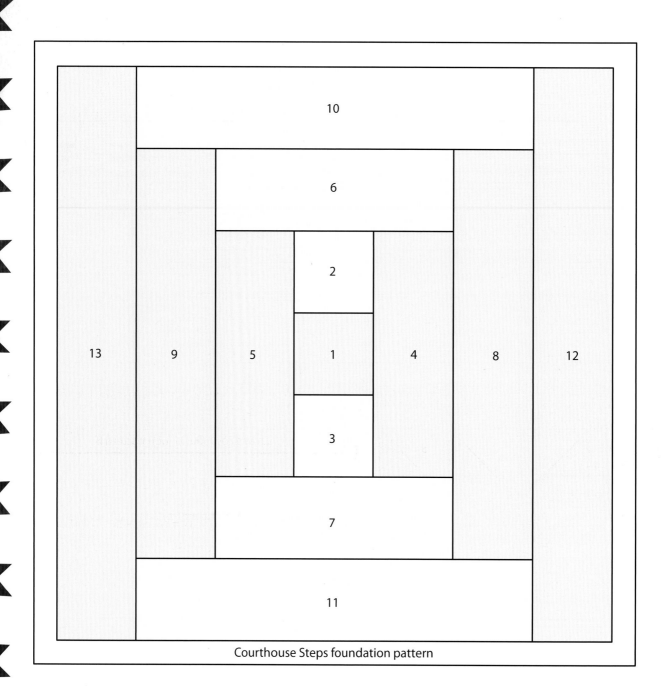

Courthouse Steps foundation pattern

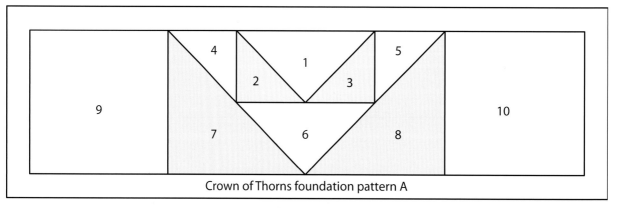

Crown of Thorns foundation pattern A

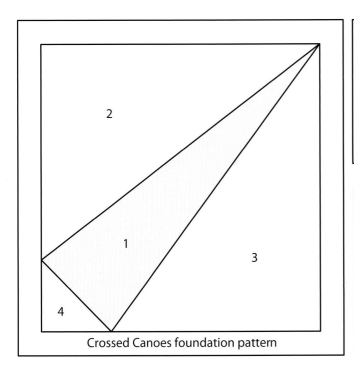

Crossed Canoes foundation pattern

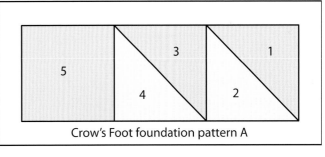

Crow's Foot foundation pattern A

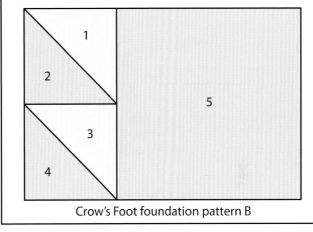

Crow's Foot foundation pattern B

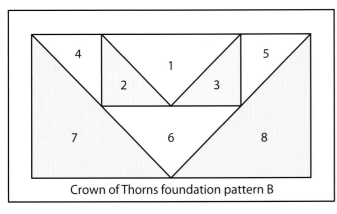

Crown of Thorns foundation pattern B

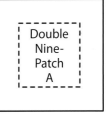

Double Nine-Patch A

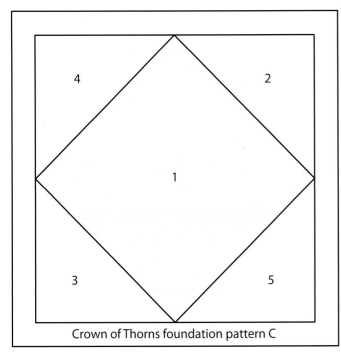

Crown of Thorns foundation pattern C

Double Nine-Patch B

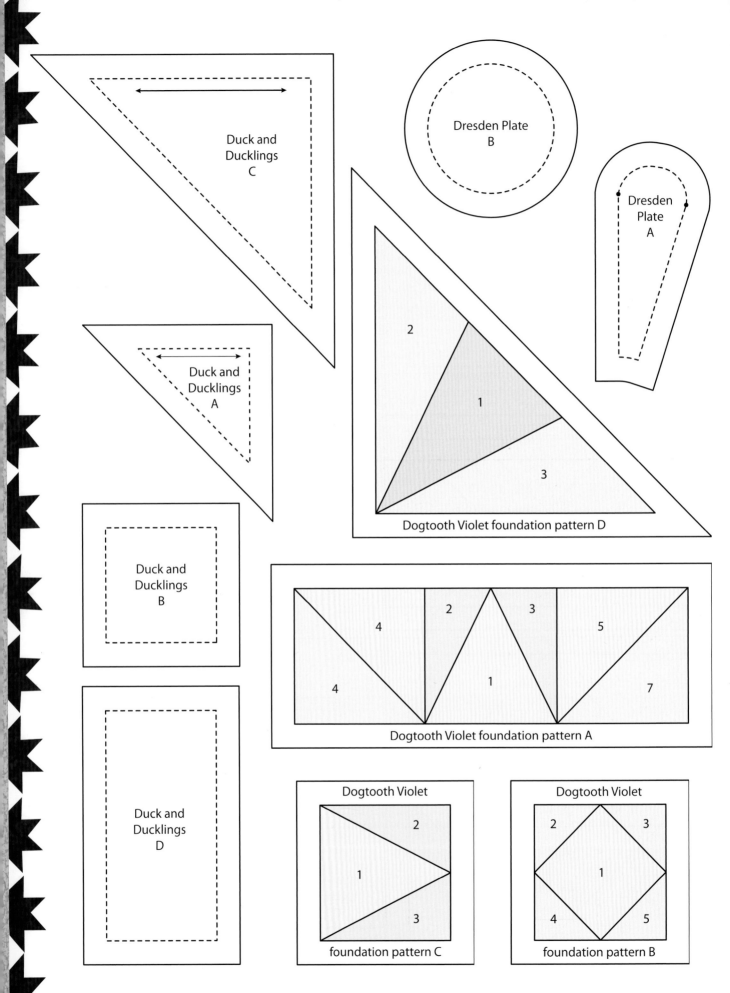

Duck and Ducklings C

Dresden Plate B

Dresden Plate A

Duck and Ducklings A

Dogtooth Violet foundation pattern D

Duck and Ducklings B

Dogtooth Violet foundation pattern A

Duck and Ducklings D

Dogtooth Violet foundation pattern C

Dogtooth Violet foundation pattern B

SYLVIA'S BRIDAL SAMPLER FROM ELM CREEK QUILTS

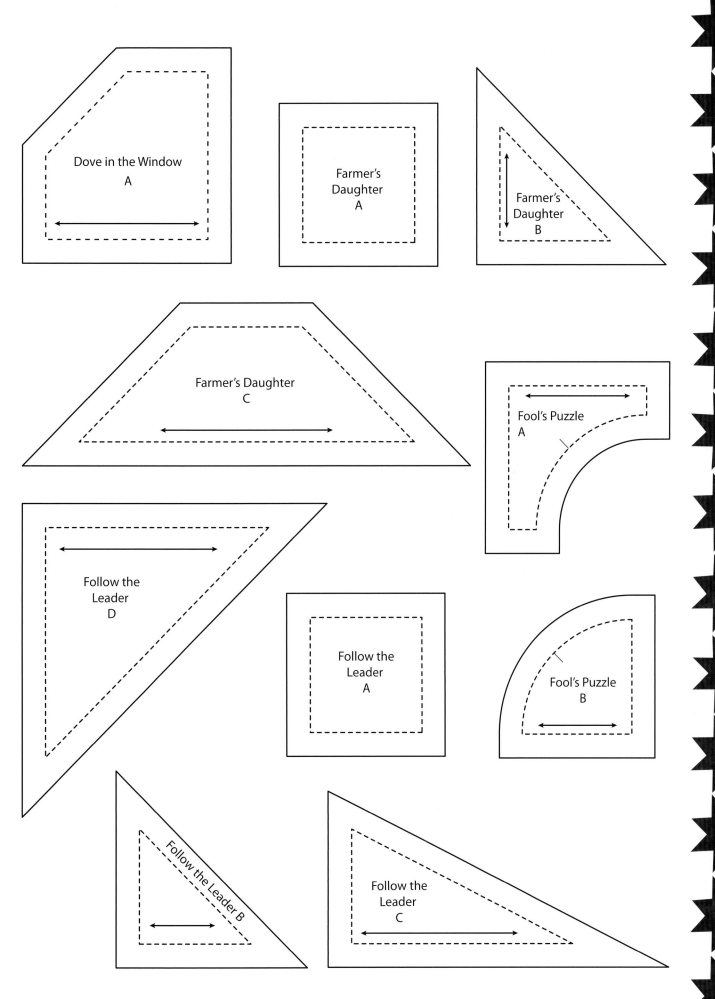

Dove in the Window
A

Farmer's
Daughter
A

Farmer's
Daughter
B

Farmer's Daughter
C

Fool's Puzzle
A

Follow the
Leader
D

Follow the
Leader
A

Fool's Puzzle
B

Follow the Leader B

Follow the
Leader
C

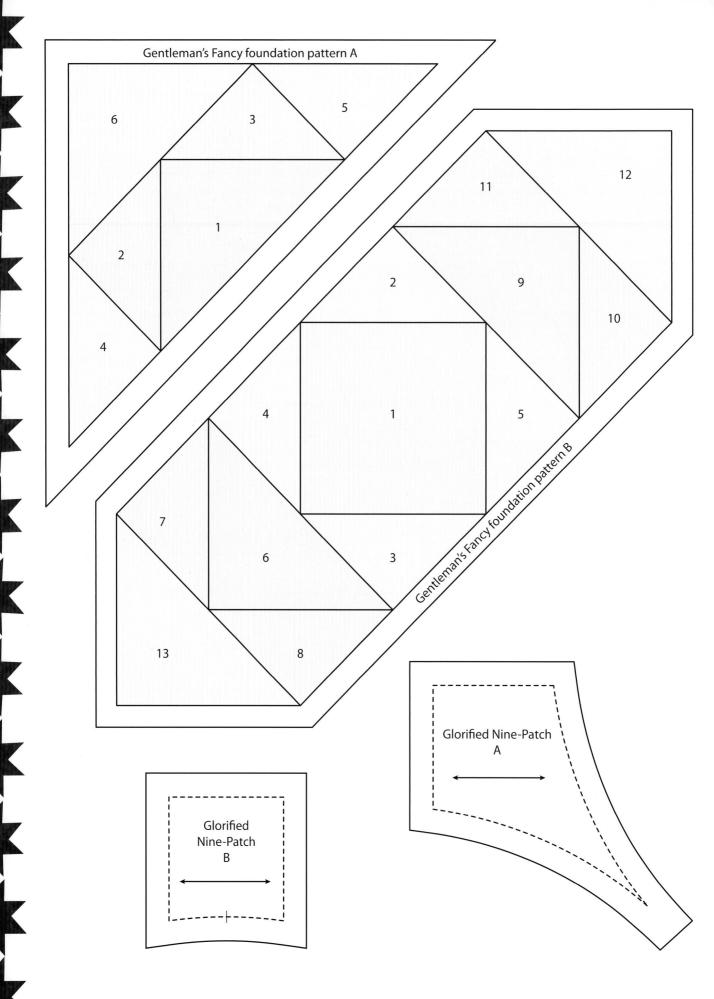

Gentleman's Fancy foundation pattern A

6
3
5
1
2
4

Gentleman's Fancy foundation pattern B

11
12
2
9
10
4
1
5
7
6
3
13
8

Glorified Nine-Patch A

Glorified Nine-Patch B

SYLVIA'S BRIDAL SAMPLER FROM ELM CREEK QUILTS

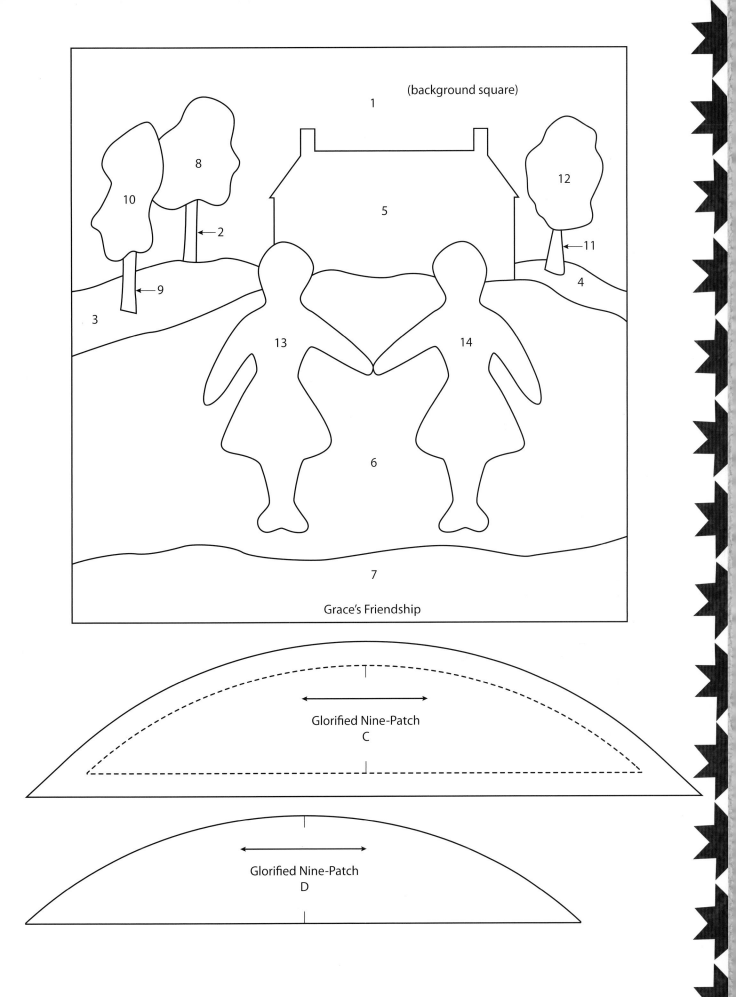

(background square)

1

8

10

12

2

5

11

9

4

3

13

14

6

7

Grace's Friendship

Glorified Nine-Patch
C

Glorified Nine-Patch
D

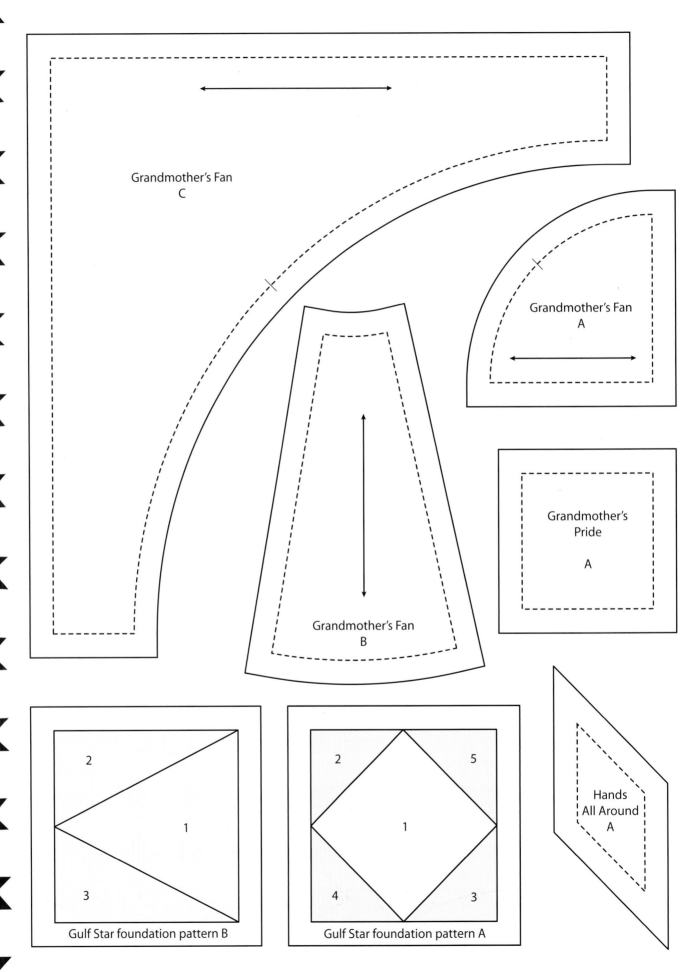

Grandmother's Fan
C

Grandmother's Fan
A

Grandmother's Fan
B

Grandmother's Pride

A

Hands
All Around
A

2

1

3

Gulf Star foundation pattern B

2

5

1

4

3

Gulf Star foundation pattern A

SYLVIA'S BRIDAL SAMPLER FROM ELM CREEK QUILTS

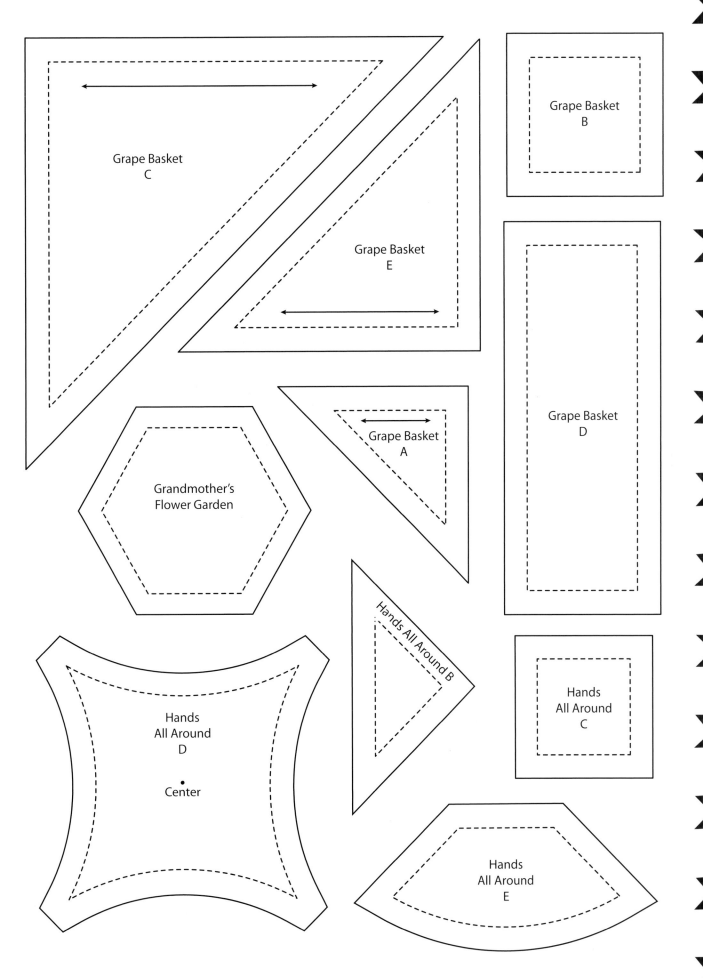

Grape Basket
C

Grape Basket
E

Grape Basket
B

Grape Basket
D

Grape Basket
A

Grandmother's
Flower Garden

Hands All Around B

Hands
All Around
C

Hands
All Around
D

• Center

Hands
All Around
E

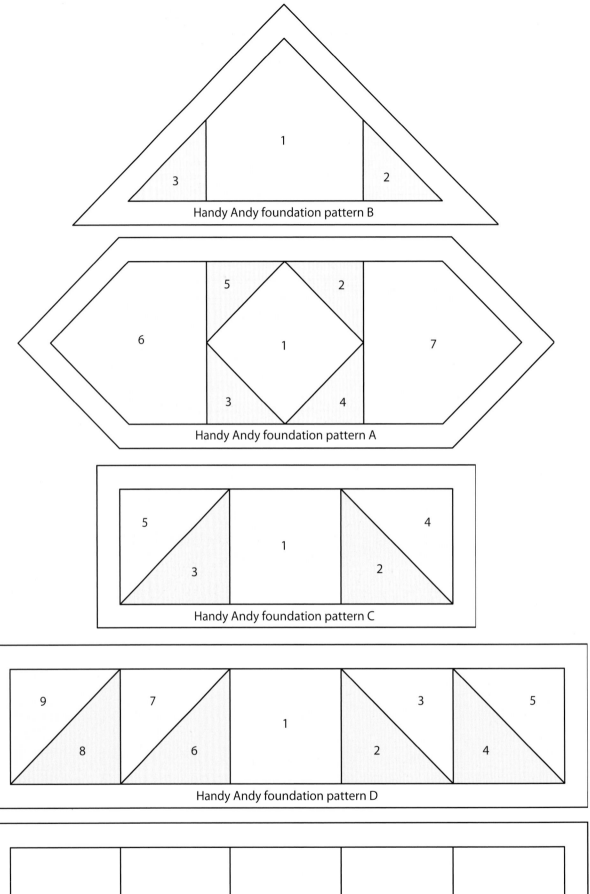

Handy Andy foundation pattern B

Handy Andy foundation pattern A

Handy Andy foundation pattern C

Handy Andy foundation pattern D

Irish Chain foundation pattern (Option 1)

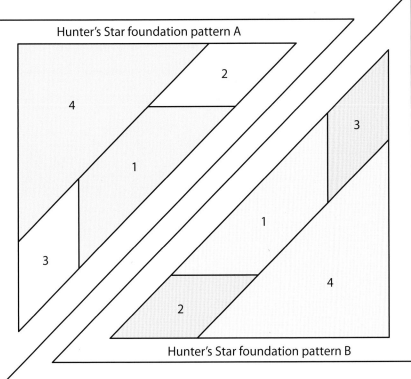

Hunter's Star foundation pattern A

2

4

1

3

3

1

4

2

Hunter's Star foundation pattern B

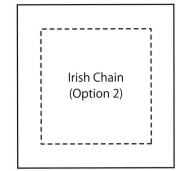

Irish Chain
(Option 2)

A

B

C

D

Indiana Rose

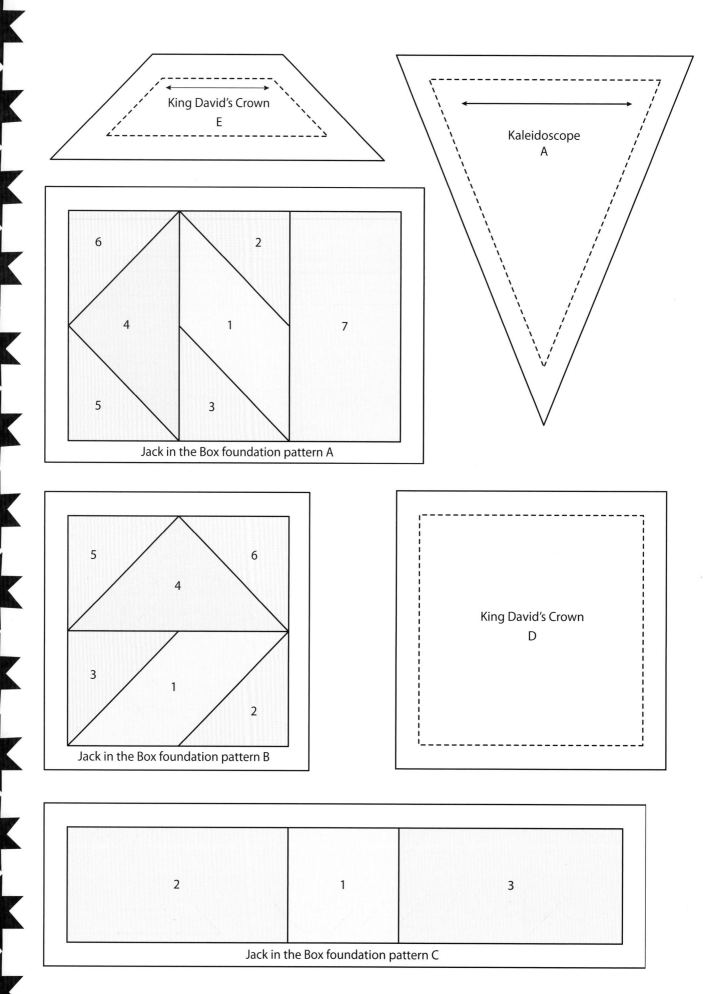

King David's Crown
E

Kaleidoscope
A

6   2

4   1   7

5   3

Jack in the Box foundation pattern A

5   4   6

3   1   2

Jack in the Box foundation pattern B

King David's Crown
D

2   1   3

Jack in the Box foundation pattern C

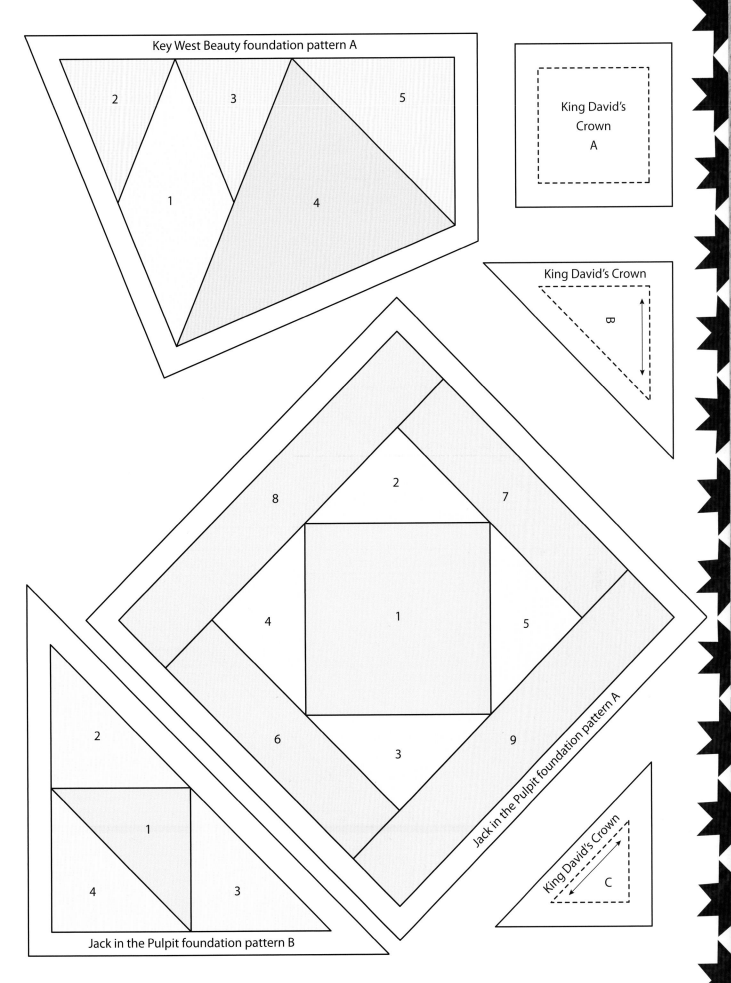

Key West Beauty foundation pattern A

King David's Crown
A

King David's Crown
B

Jack in the Pulpit foundation pattern A

King David's Crown
C

Jack in the Pulpit foundation pattern B

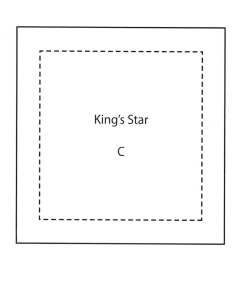

King's Star

C

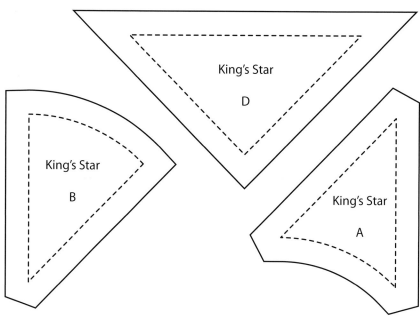

King's Star

D

King's Star

B

King's Star

A

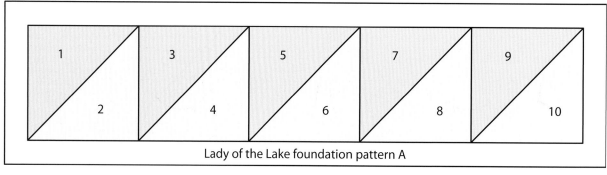

| 1 | 3 | 5 | 7 | 9 |
| 2 | 4 | 6 | 8 | 10 |

Lady of the Lake foundation pattern A

Lady of the Lake foundation pattern B

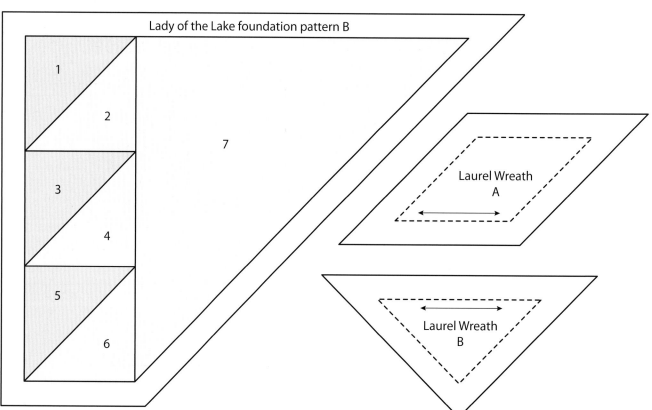

1
2
3
4
5
6
7

Laurel Wreath
A

Laurel Wreath
B

Lancaster Rose

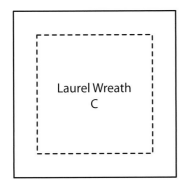

Laurel Wreath
C

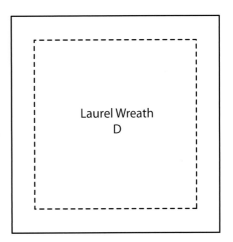

Laurel Wreath
D

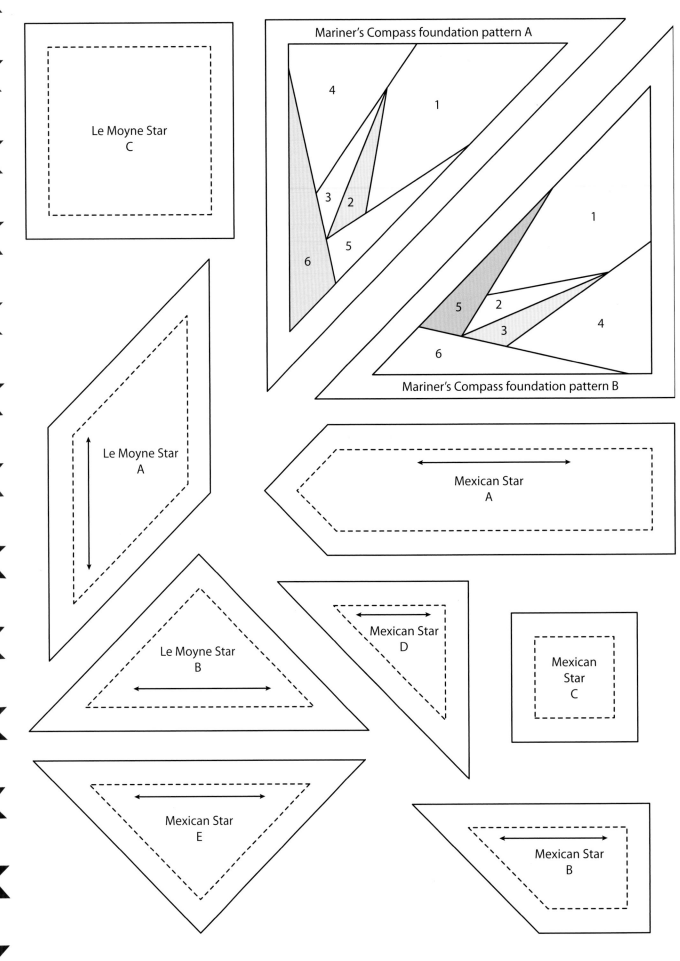

Le Moyne Star
C

Mariner's Compass foundation pattern A

4

1

3

2

5

6

1

5

2

3

4

6

Mariner's Compass foundation pattern B

Le Moyne Star
A

Mexican Star
A

Le Moyne Star
B

Mexican Star
D

Mexican
Star
C

Mexican Star
E

Mexican Star
B

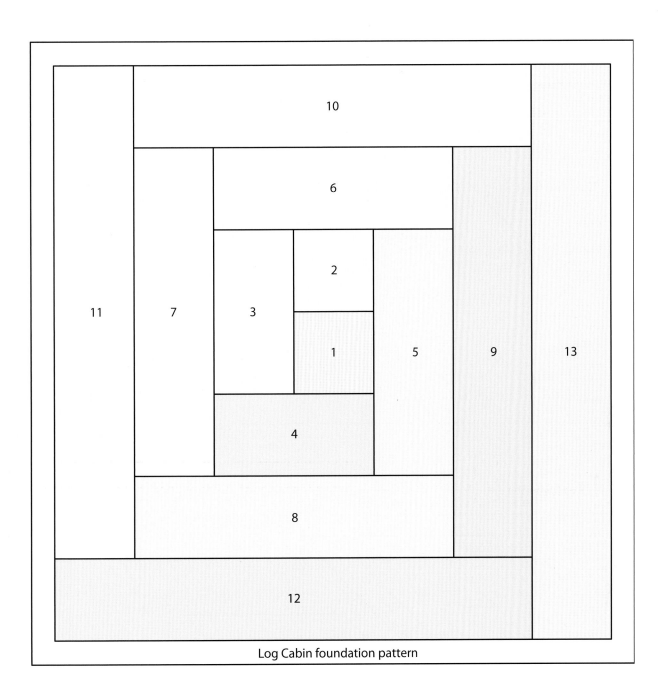

Log Cabin foundation pattern

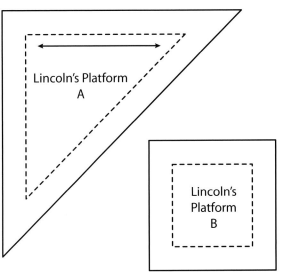

Lincoln's Platform
A

Lincoln's
Platform
B

Lincoln's Platform
C

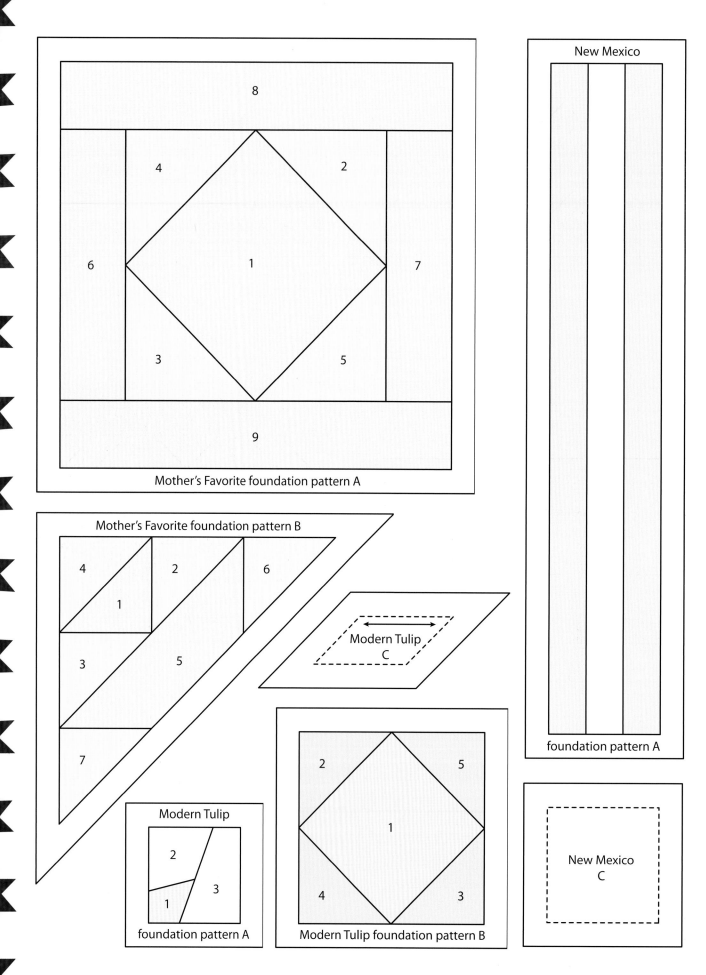

New Mexico

Mother's Favorite foundation pattern A

Mother's Favorite foundation pattern B

Modern Tulip
C

foundation pattern A

Modern Tulip

foundation pattern A

Modern Tulip foundation pattern B

New Mexico
C

SYLVIA'S BRIDAL SAMPLER FROM ELM CREEK QUILTS

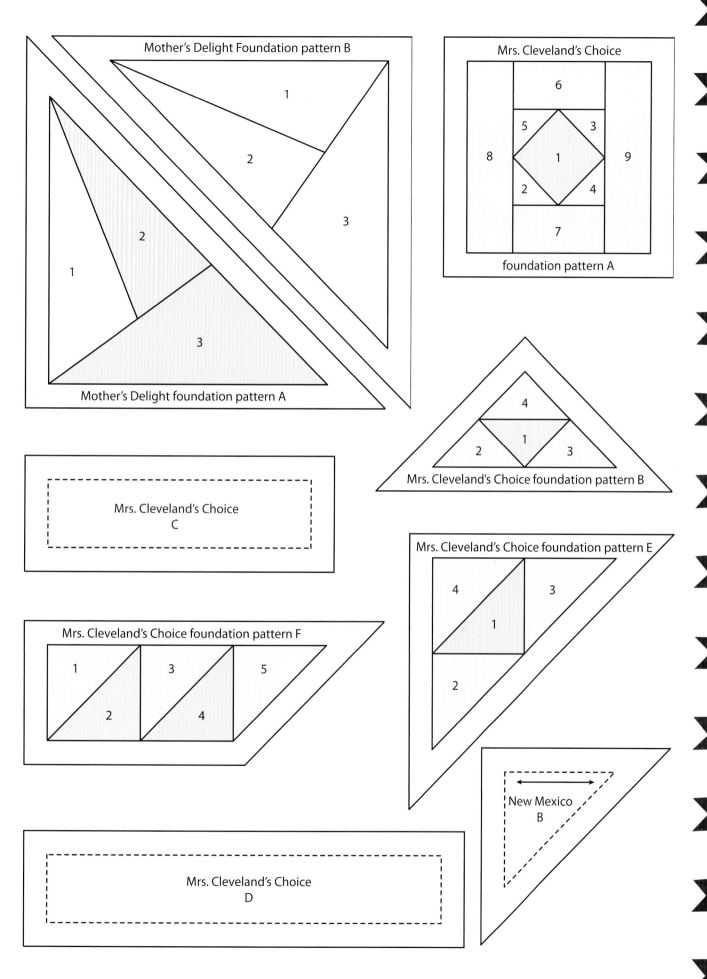

Mother's Delight Foundation pattern B

1

2

3

Mrs. Cleveland's Choice

6

5   3

8   1   9

2   4

7

foundation pattern A

Mother's Delight foundation pattern A

1

2

3

4

1

2   3

Mrs. Cleveland's Choice foundation pattern B

Mrs. Cleveland's Choice
C

Mrs. Cleveland's Choice foundation pattern E

4   3

1

2

Mrs. Cleveland's Choice foundation pattern F

1   3   5

2   4

New Mexico
B

Mrs. Cleveland's Choice
D

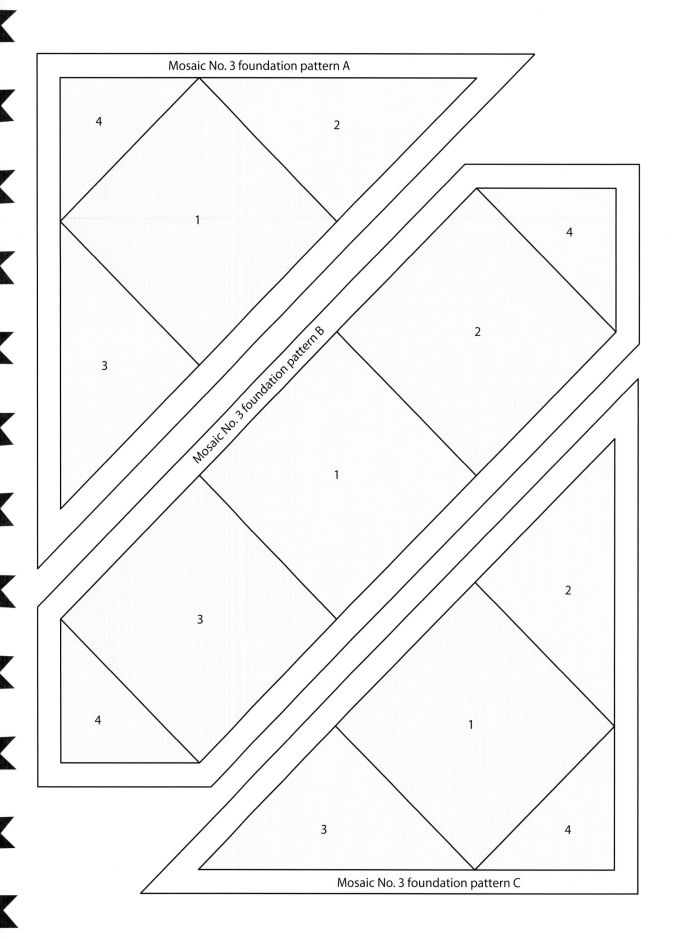

Mosaic No. 3 foundation pattern A

Mosaic No. 3 foundation pattern B

Mosaic No. 3 foundation pattern C

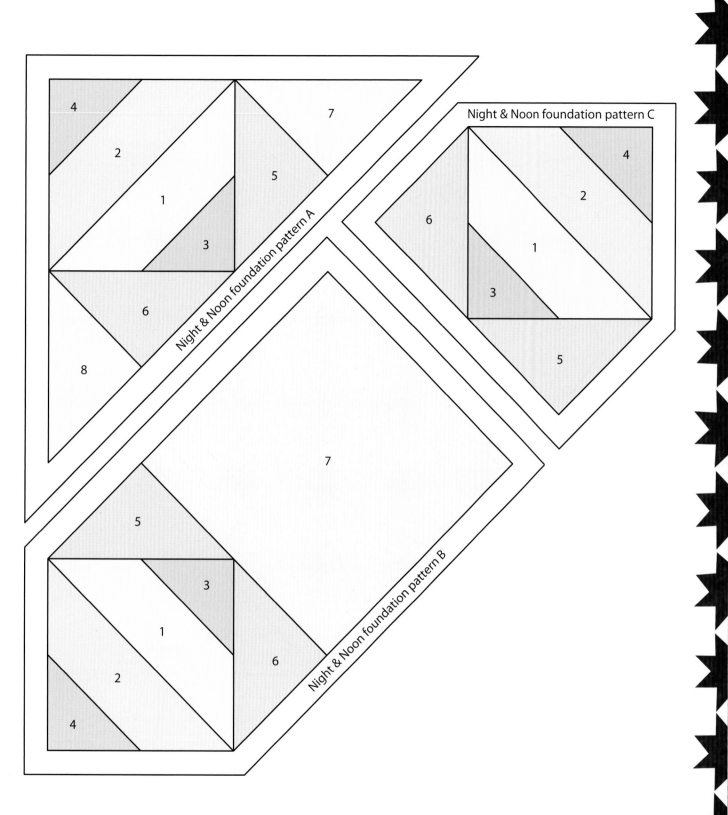

Night & Noon foundation pattern A

Night & Noon foundation pattern B

Night & Noon foundation pattern C

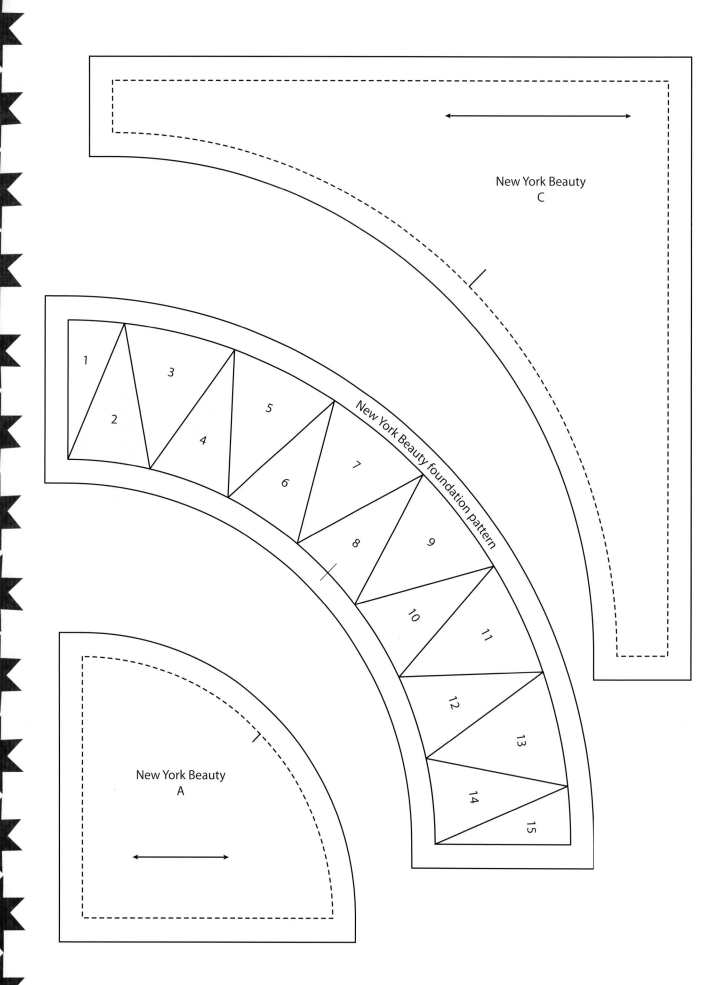

New York Beauty
C

New York Beauty foundation pattern

1
2
3
4
5
6
7
8
9
10
11
12
13
14
15

New York Beauty
A

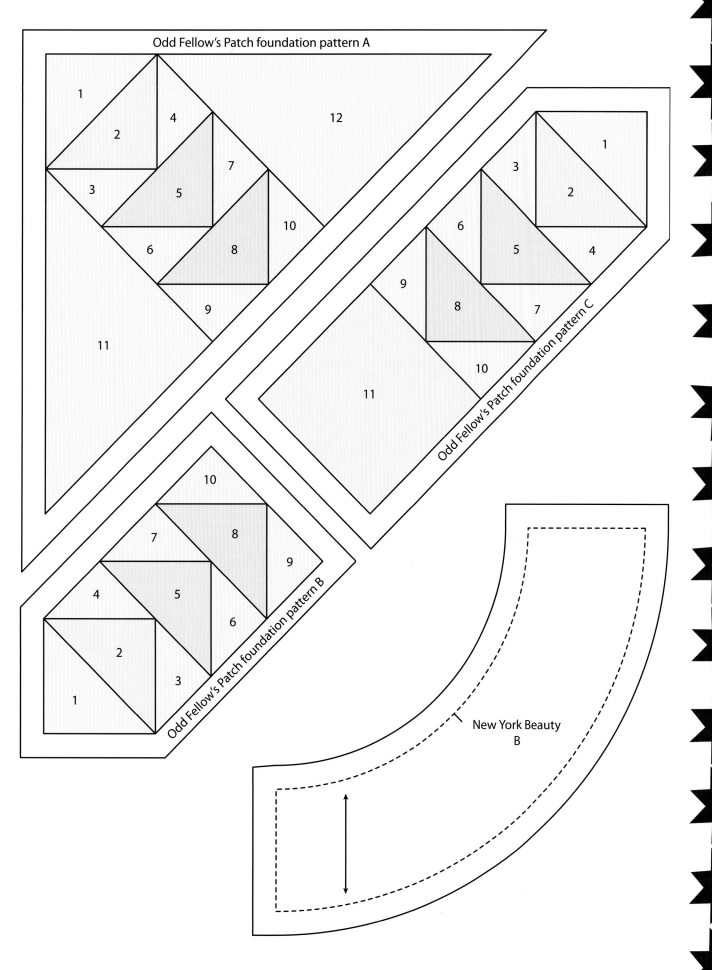

Odd Fellow's Patch foundation pattern A

Odd Fellow's Patch foundation pattern C

Odd Fellow's Patch foundation pattern B

New York Beauty
B

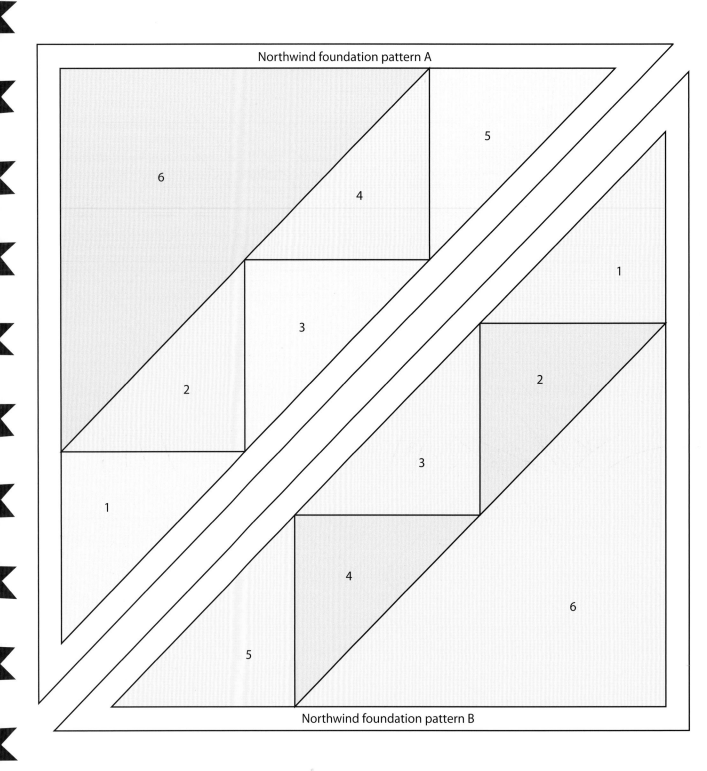

Northwind foundation pattern A

Northwind foundation pattern B

SYLVIA'S BRIDAL SAMPLER FROM ELM CREEK QUILTS

Oklahoma Dogwood
B

Orange Peel
B

Oklahoma Dogwood foundation pattern

1 2 3 4 5 6 7 8 9 10 11 12 13

Orange Peel
A

Oklahoma Dogwood
A

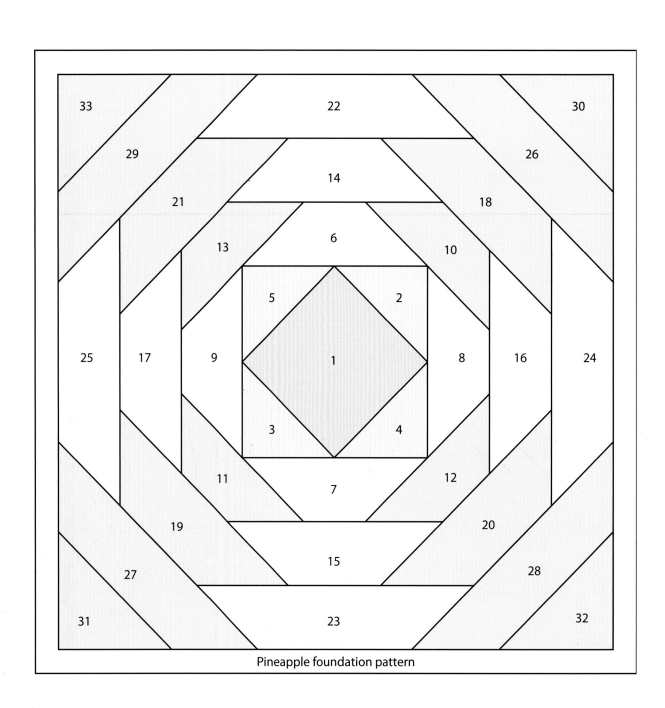

Pineapple foundation pattern

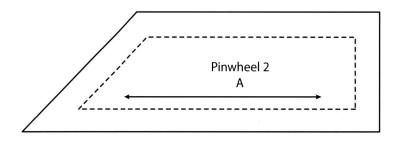

Pinwheel 2
A

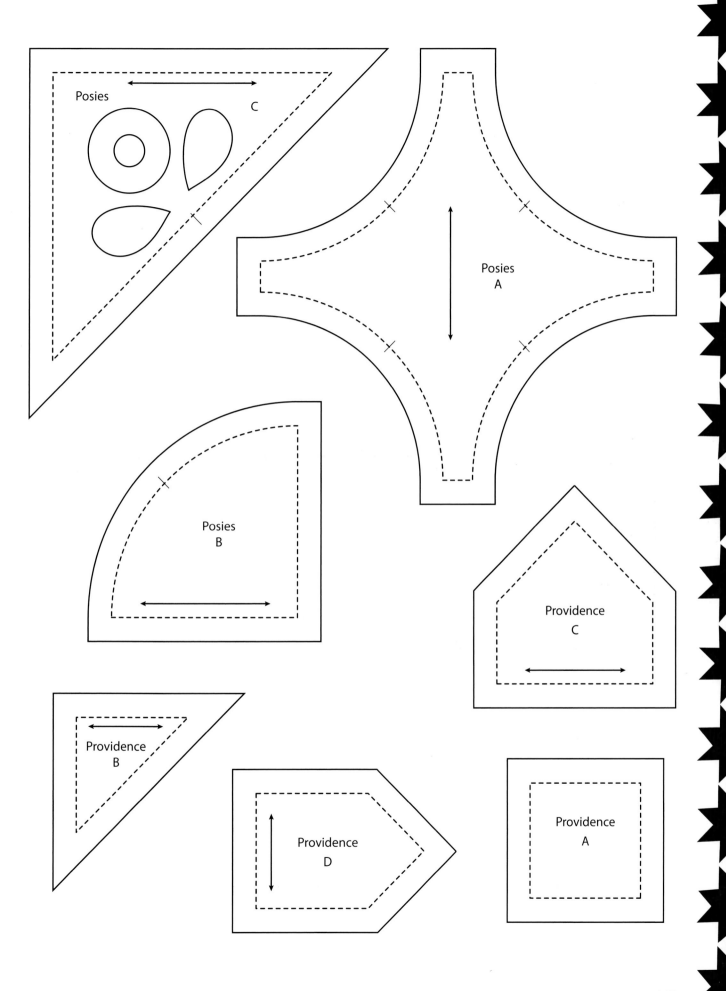

Posies C

Posies A

Posies B

Providence C

Providence B

Providence D

Providence A

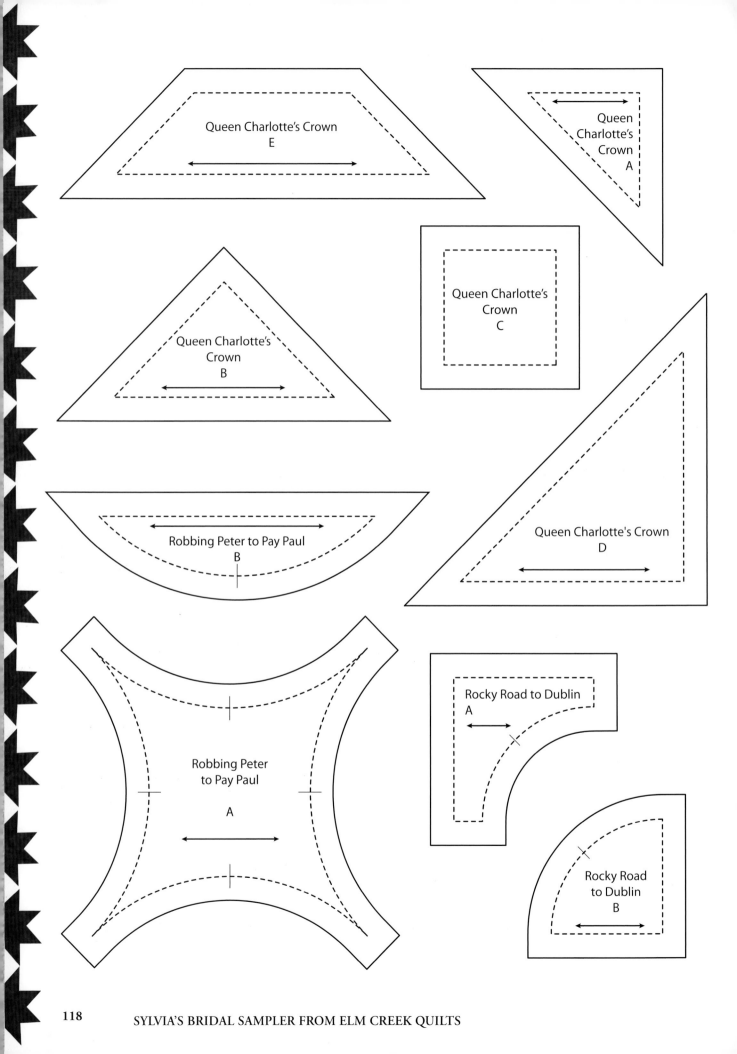

Queen Charlotte's Crown
E

Queen Charlotte's Crown
A

Queen Charlotte's Crown
C

Queen Charlotte's Crown
B

Robbing Peter to Pay Paul
B

Queen Charlotte's Crown
D

Robbing Peter to Pay Paul
A

Rocky Road to Dublin
A

Rocky Road to Dublin
B

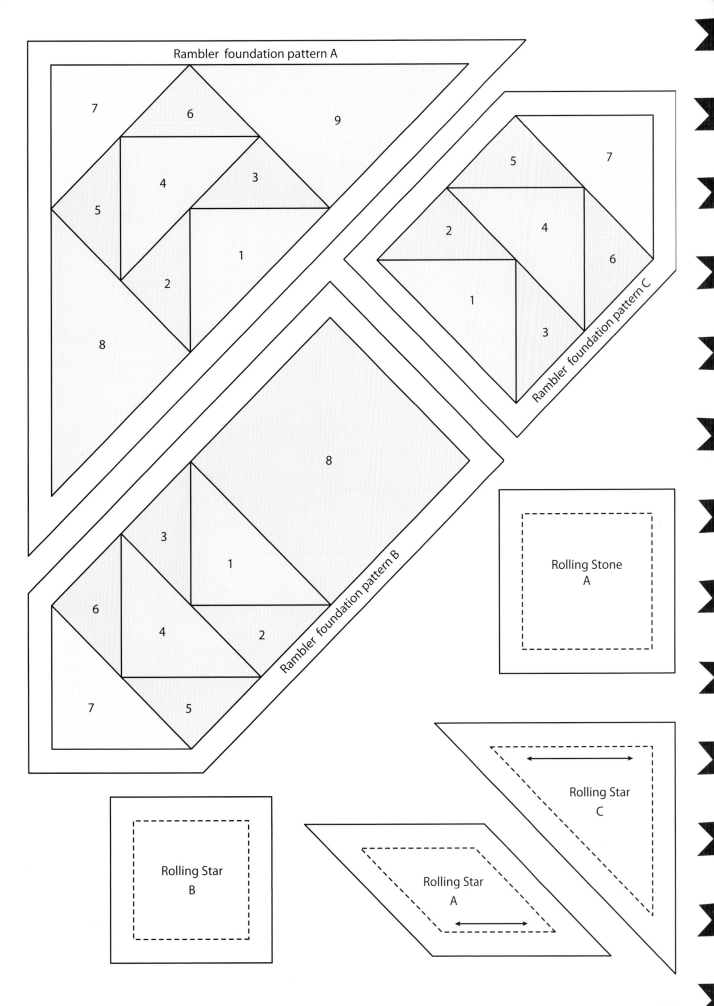

Rambler foundation pattern A

7 6 9

4 3

5

1

2

8

Rambler foundation pattern C

5 7

2 4

6

1

3

Rambler foundation pattern B

8

3 1

6 2

4

7 5

Rolling Stone
A

Rolling Star
C

Rolling Star
B

Rolling Star
A

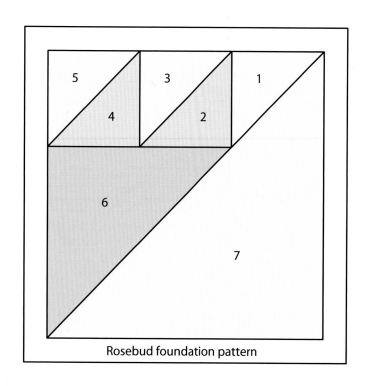

Rosebud foundation pattern

Silver and Gold
B

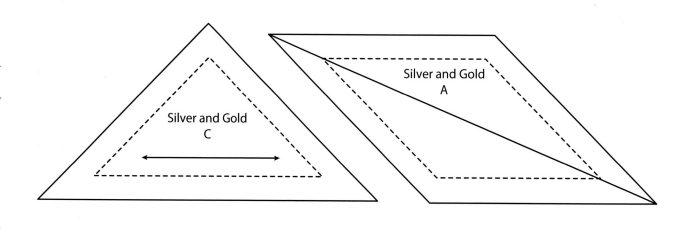

Silver and Gold
C

Silver and Gold
A

Sarah's
Favorite
A

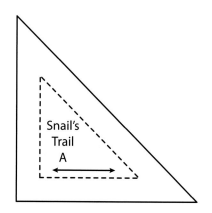

Snail's
Trail
A

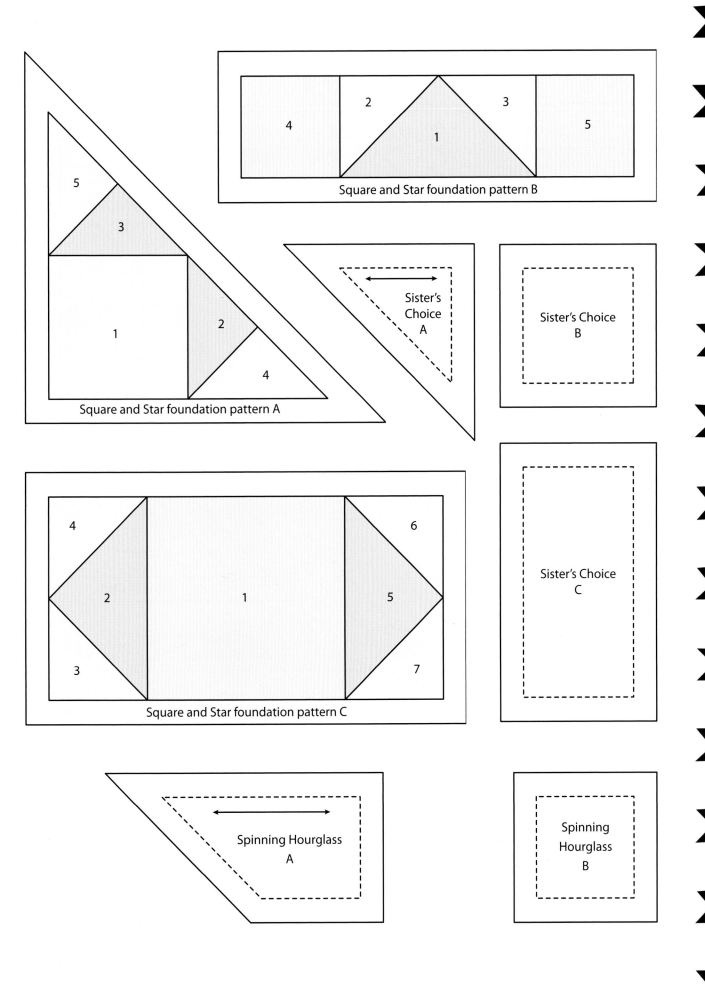

Square and Star foundation pattern B

Square and Star foundation pattern A

Sister's Choice A

Sister's Choice B

Square and Star foundation pattern C

Sister's Choice C

Spinning Hourglass A

Spinning Hourglass B

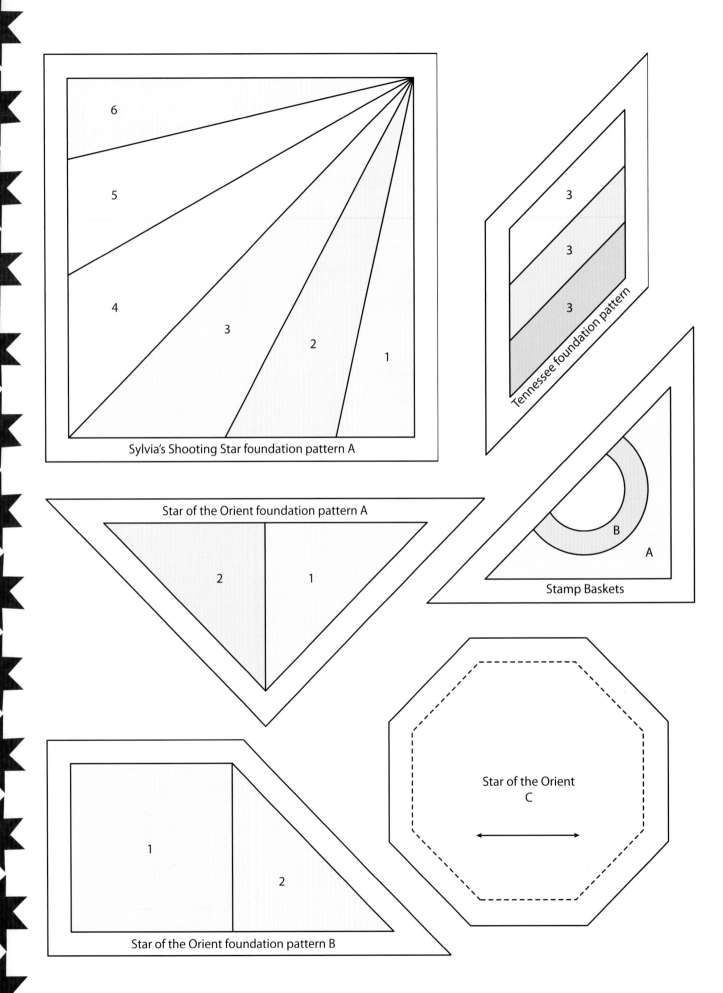

6

5

4

3

2

1

Sylvia's Shooting Star foundation pattern A

3

3

3

Tennessee foundation pattern

Star of the Orient foundation pattern A

2

1

B

A

Stamp Baskets

Star of the Orient
C

1

2

Star of the Orient foundation pattern B

True Lover's
Knot
A

Tennessee
A

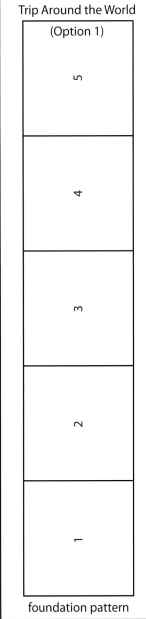

Trip Around the World
(Option 1)

5

4

3

2

1

foundation pattern

True Lover's Knot
B

Tennessee
B

The Friendship Quilt foundation pattern

4

2

1

3

5

Trip Around
the World
(Option 2)
A

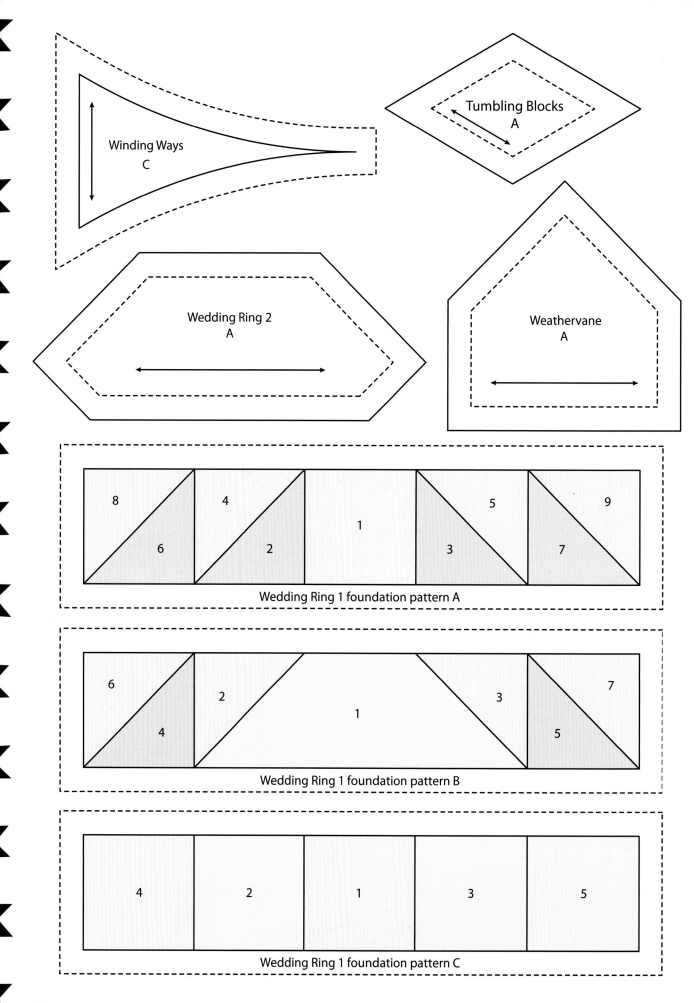

Winding Ways
C

Tumbling Blocks
A

Wedding Ring 2
A

Weathervane
A

Wedding Ring 1 foundation pattern A

Wedding Ring 1 foundation pattern B

Wedding Ring 1 foundation pattern C

SYLVIA'S BRIDAL SAMPLER FROM ELM CREEK QUILTS

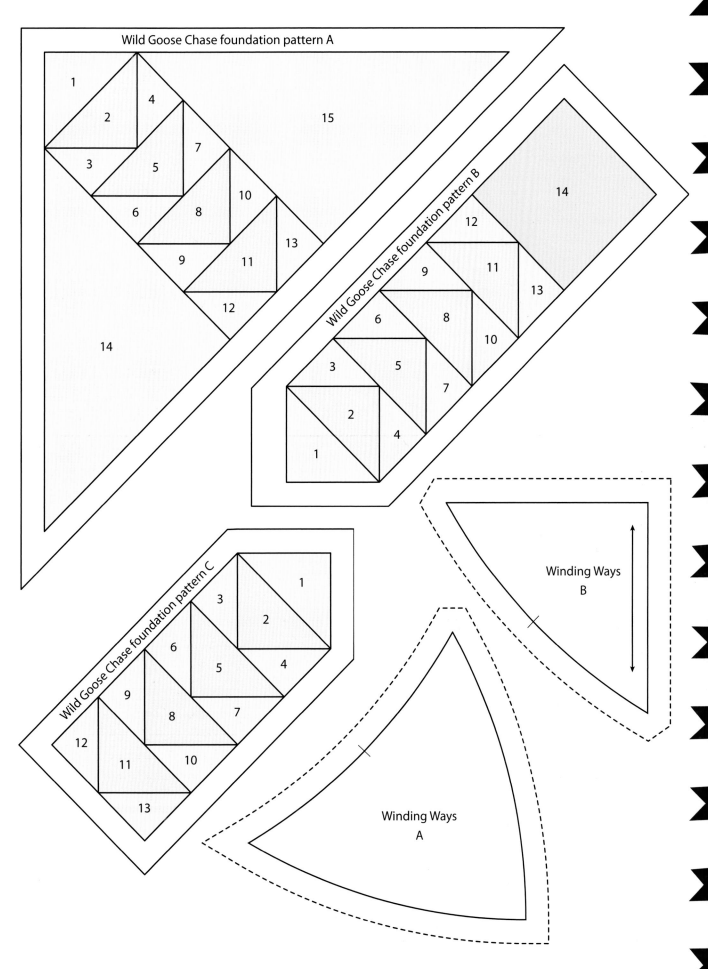

Wild Goose Chase foundation pattern A

Wild Goose Chase foundation pattern B

Wild Goose Chase foundation pattern C

Winding Ways
B

Winding Ways
A

Block Index

About the Author

Jennifer Chiaverini, a graduate of the University of Notre Dame and the University of Chicago, taught writing at Pennsylvania State University and Edgewood College before leaving teaching to write full-time. The author of the popular Elm Creek Quilts novels and the first companion book of quilt patterns, *Elm Creek Quilts: Quilt Projects Inspired by the Elm Creek Quilts Novels*, Chiaverini is also the designer of the Elm Creek Quilts fabric lines for Red Rooster Fabrics. A frequent lecturer at quilt shows and writing conferences, Chiaverini lives in Madison, Wisconsin, with her husband and two sons.

Also by Jennifer Chiaverini

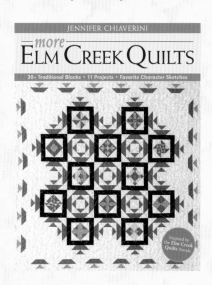

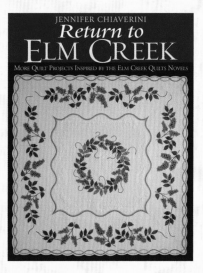

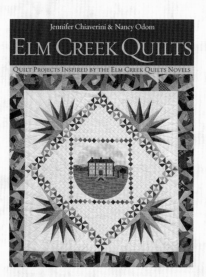

For a list of other fine books from C&T Publishing, ask for a free catalog:

C&T Publishing, Inc.
P.O. Box 1456
Lafayette, CA 94549
(800) 284-1114
Email: ctinfo@ctpub.com
Website: www.ctpub.com

C&T Publishing's professional photography services are now available to the public.
Visit us at www.ctmediaservices.com.

For quilting supplies:

Cotton Patch
1025 Brown Ave.
Lafayette, CA 94549
Store: (925) 284-1177
Mail order: (925) 283-7883
Email: CottonPa@aol.com
Website: www.quiltusa.com

Note: Fabrics used in the quilts shown may not be currently available, as fabric manufacturers keep most fabrics in print for only a short time.

Great Titles from

C&T PUBLISHING